The Thou of Nature

The Thou of Nature

Religious Naturalism and Reverence for Sentient Life

Donald A. Crosby

Cover image © Anke Seidlitz/www.kolibriphotography.com

Published by State University of New York Press, Albany

© 2013 State University of New York

For information, contact State University of New York Press, Albany, NY
www.sunypress.edu

Production by Diane Ganeles
Marketing by Kate McDonnell

Library of Congress Cataloging-in-Publication Data

Crosby, Donald A.
    The thou of nature : religious naturalism and reverence for sentient life / Donald A. Crosby.
        pages cm
    Includes bibliographical references and index.
    ISBN 978-1-4384-4669-1 (hc : alk. paper)—978-1-4384-4670-7 (pb : alk. paper)
    1. Philosophy of nature.   2. Human ecology—Religious aspects.   I. Title.

    BD581.C765 2013
    202'.12—dc23   2012026095

10 9 8 7 6 5 4 3 2 1

For Bathsheba
Cat, Companion, and Wondrous Creature of Nature

Contents

Preface

This book follows upon two earlier books devoted to presentation and discussion of the version of religious naturalism I term *Religion of Nature*. The first one, simply entitled *A Religion of Nature* (2002), laid out and defended the main outlines of the metaphysical and religious aspects of this outlook, while the second one, *Living with Ambiguity: Religious Naturalism and the Menace of Evil* (2008), focused on its interpretations of and responses to the persistent presence of evil in ourselves and in the world. The present book further expands the focus and concerns of Religion of Nature. It does so by dealing with our relations as humans to the massive numbers of other living beings who inhabit this planet with us and especially to those of their number that are, like us, capable of at least some measure of conscious awareness and feeling and can accordingly be referred to as fellow *thous*. The book's subtitle refers to the latter as *sentient* forms of life.

The main title of this book *The Thou of Nature* calls attention to the fact that earthly nature is a community of thous of many different kinds of which we humans are an integral part and on whose continuing prosperity and well-being we cannot help but critically rely. The nonhuman thous in their turn are keenly dependent on the respect, care, compassion, cooperation, and protection of us human beings. Thus, nature here on earth is not just a mere assemblage of external objects, instruments, or automata set over against us humans as its sole true subjects and subservient to our every presumed need, use, or whim. I contend throughout this volume that recognizing and responding appropriately to the ubiquitous thou (or sentient) aspect of nature has profound religious as well as moral significance, a significance that is becoming increasingly and inescapably apparent in the gravely imperiled ecological circumstances of the contemporary world.

I begin the book by studying the effects of three major scientific revolutions of the past four centuries on our conception of the status and role of human beings in nature, namely, the cosmological, evolutionary, and ecological revolutions. The full significance of these three revolutions, I maintain, is only gradually seeping into our consciousness and modes of behavior. I then present evidence—much of it recently discovered and brought into view—for the thesis that consciousness awareness is not restricted to humans but is widely dispersed, albeit in varying degrees, among nonhuman forms life. I proceed to draw out the consequences of this thesis for our moral and religious outlook toward and treatment of the innumerable creatures of earth that belong to species other than our own.

I show that these creatures, and especially those capable of conscious awareness and feeling, are richly deserving of our moral recognition, respect, and responsibility. They therefore qualify for and are entitled to treatment in accordance with six presumptive natural rights that relate to their well-being, their distinctive natures, and the integrity of their natural environments. In showing this to be so, I draw alternatively and when appropriate throughout the book on the language of rights, of utility, and of what relates to the particular *telos* or characteristic mode of life and development of different nonhuman life forms. These three languages, reflecting three different types of ethical theory, can each contribute in its own way to our understanding of our ethical obligations to nonhuman animals, and there is no need, in my judgment, for making any of the three subordinate to or reducible to only one of them.

I agree generally with ethical philosopher Edmund L. Pincoffs that "the field of moral problems is so large and various that the narrow subfields picked out by ethical theories fail to include most of what they should include."[1] I would replace "most" with "much" in his statement, however, because I am convinced that each of the standard theories involved in ethical discussions among philosophers does cover a lot of the relevant ground, even though none of them encompasses all of that ground. There is plenty of room, in other words, for alternative theories that can complement one another and help to compensate for one another's deficiencies—each casting its special light on the immense field of existing and emerging moral problems and concerns. I do not enter here into the details of discussion, criticism, or defense of such theories but simply draw on the language of one or more of them as seems appropriate in particular contexts. I hope that resolutely theory-minded philosophers and colleagues are willing to make allowances for my procedure in this regard. That sort of high-level theoretical discussion certainly has its place, but I have not deemed it to be necessary here. I make further reference to this issue in Chapter 7.

In addition, I make a case for the thesis that the abundant nonhuman animals on earth are sacred beings within the sacredness of nature as a whole and should elicit from us humans profound responses of reverence and awe. There is thus a fundamental religious as well as moral dimension to our appropriate attitude toward them. I pay special attention to the topic of *empowerment* in Religion of Nature, as over against its other two essential aspects of *assurance* and *demand*, and show how and why this empowerment is closely connected with our place on earth and our treatment of the other creatures of earth.

The rights of some creatures obviously can and do come into conflict with the rights of others, however, and such conflicts can be particularly problematic and glaring in the frequent situations that involve oppositions between the rights of a burgeoning and encroaching human population and the rights of the multifarious nonhuman forms of life on earth. I take such conflicts under consideration and discuss ways of regarding and dealing with them. This discussion is a prominent motif throughout the book.

It underlies and informs my approaches to hunting and fishing, eating and wearing, and other areas of responsibility and concern such as animal experimentation; rodeos, circuses, zoos, and aquariums; endangered species; the human population explosion; and the threat of global climate change. I observe that some cases of conflict can be more easily resolved than others, and that the more vexing, difficult, or complex of them need to be approached on a case-by-case basis. For example, I argue that rodeos, circuses, zoos, and aquariums should be phased out and closed down, but that animal experimentation, especially that for the avowed sake of detecting and preventing human diseases, while in need of careful analysis and monitoring, does not admit of such wholesale condemnation. Aspects of it need to be brought to an end; other aspects do not, at least at present.

I present what I consider to be compelling reasons in support of the position that sport hunting and fishing cannot be morally or religiously justified when their sole or overriding purpose is killing animals for fun, challenge, or alleged human inspiration, and I respond to objections to this position. I analyze in some detail and argue against the many abuses of current factory farming and industrial fishing practices, and I set forth arguments in favor of vegetarianism as an alternative to the consumption of meat. I also contend against procuring, wearing, and using such animal products as skins, furs, feathers, or tusks for apparel, ornamentation, or other purposes, on the ground that their procurement inflicts suffering and death on animals and that many quite satisfactory substitutes for these products are now readily available.

I consider and reject the contention that my views, if put into practice, would amount to a recipe for widespread economic disruption and even chaos. I respond throughout the book to the anticipated more general protest that my view of these and other matters is hopelessly idealistic, impractical, and utopian. I also respond to the expected charge from some quarters that my outlook on nonhuman animals and my prescriptions for their treatment are embarrassingly romantic, sentimental, and anthropocentric.

I bring the book to a conclusion with an eightfold set of general principles and prescriptions. This set is proposed as a summary of my view of how Religion of Nature conceives of our relation to members of other species of animal life, but I think that its vision applies, at least in spirit if not in every detail, to many other religious (and moral) outlooks as well. If we humans can determine to devote ourselves to an ardent, sustained search for ways to put this set of basic principles and prescriptions—and the major themes and arguments of this book they reflect—into practice, we could bring about a revolution in thinking and acting that would contribute immeasurably to the welfare and flourishing of all of earth's creatures, including ourselves.

I want to acknowledge my indebtedness to two friends who graciously read and commented on an earlier version of some parts of this book: philosopher/theologian David E. Conner and entomologist Jeffrey A. Lockwood. Both brought into view important aspects of my thinking that needed modification and improvement, and they registered disagreements with some of my views that required that I reevaluate these views, analyze them more thoroughly, or defend them more convincingly. Two anonymous readers commissioned by State University of New York Press have also made helpful criticisms and suggestions concerning an earlier draft of this book, and I have endeavored to take them into account by clarifying my views, altering those views when appropriate, or strengthening the arguments I make on behalf of particular claims. I am grateful to these four commentators for their thoughtful responses to some my ideas and contentions. The positions I have finally taken and defended are of course my responsibility, not theirs.

I also want to express my appreciation to my longtime colleague and esteemed friend, philosopher, and animal ethicist Bernard E. Rollin. Rollin has worked tirelessly and with great effectiveness in his teaching, writing, and speaking—the latter throughout the world, on numerous occasions, and with many different kinds of audience, including veterinarians, farmers, ranchers, and legislators as well as philosophers—to articulate and defend the rights of nonhuman animals for compassionate and humane treatment. I have learned much and gained much inspiration from his friendship, his example, his books and articles, and the many stimulating conversations we have had over the years. Finally, I am grateful to my wife Pam whose lifelong deep sensitivity to issues of animal mistreatment, suffering, and deprivation has helped to arouse and strengthen in me similar attitudes and concerns.

1

Religious Naturalism and Three Scientific Revolutions

If we choose to let conjecture run wild, then animals—our fellow brethren in pain, disease, death, suffering and famine, our slaves in the most laborious works, our companions in our amusements—they may partake from our origin in one common ancestor, we may be all netted together.

—Charles Darwin[1]

Introduction

Religion has many faces. There are the great world religions and the different modes of interpretation and practice within each of them. There are the pervasive religious motifs, rites, and undergirdings of tribal cultures. There are monotheistic religions, religions of two deities, and religions of multiple deities. The deities can be perceived as radically transcendent, radically immanent, or somewhere in-between. In some quarters there is even the covert worship of Satan or other powers of evil. There are also religions in which there are no deities or in which deities are subordinate to some more ultimate principle or power. And there is a movement of thought and action called religious naturalism, of which I and a growing number of persons, especially in the United States, are adherents and proponents. This book will concentrate on an extremely important and demanding aspect of wholehearted commitment to religious naturalism, that is, the import of such a commitment for attitudes and actions of human beings in their relations to other forms of life here on earth.

Religious naturalism, as I and many others interpret it, has no belief in or devotion to God, Goddess, gods, or goddesses. For it, nature in some shape or form is all there is, ever has been, or ever will be. Nothing else lies before it, behind it, or beyond it as its ultimate ground, source, sustainer, or guide. Nature exists and persists by virtue of its own inherent, self-contained potentialities, principles, and laws. There is no alleged independent realm of the supernatural and no special, higher revelations of truth or value coming from such a realm. There is no avowed supernatural basis for help in time of need, for transformation of life, or for coping with the threats and exigencies of finite existence.

In at least some of the forms of religious naturalism, the present state of nature, or nature natured (*natura naturata*), is produced and underlaid by the irrepressively creative (but also by this same token perennially destructive) presence and power of nature naturing (*natura naturans*) that gives rise to all that has been, is now, and ever shall be, and that transforms what has already been into what is yet to come. Nature is thus not a static system but a restlessly dynamic one, undergoing radical changes over long periods, its creations and its destructions going hand-in-hand. A massive star exploded, for example, enabling our solar system to be born, and the prolific biological evolution here on earth that has given rise to us humans and diverse other forms of life has littered its waysides with extinct species.

In the perspective of religious naturalism, human beings are integral parts of nature, one particular species of life amid the vast numbers of such species and their members that presently dwell or have previously dwelt on this planet. Humans are linked with all other creatures in a common evolutionary history based on a common DNA template, and they are bound together with them in intimate, crucial relations of ecological dependency. For religious naturalism, there is no promise of a blissful continuing life for individual humans beyond the grave. Individual humans must eventually die just as members of all other species of life on earth must. They have no immortal souls; their mental and spiritual capacities are functions of their complex living bodies. And there is no credible basis of hope for the future resurrection of their bodies.

Despite these and other features that sharply demarcate it from the theistic religions so familiar to us in the Western world, religious naturalism strongly supports and urges a fundamental type of distinctively religious commitment, namely, commitment to *nature itself* as the fit focus of profound religious awe and devotion, and as the ultimate source of religious assurance, demand, and empowerment. It is neither pan*theistic* nor panen*theistic*, however, because there is no *theos* or deity of any sort involved.

I have developed and defended a version of religious naturalism and its implications for thought and life in other writings,[2] but I want now to address the meanings it can have for the character and comportment of our lives in communion with nonhuman lives, the profuse lives we are privileged to have surrounding us on every side and for whom in the perspective of my own version of religious naturalism—or what I shall henceforth term *Religion of Nature*—we humans have urgent and compelling responsibilities. These responsibilities, as properly acknowledged, challenge us to experience, conceive, and put increasingly into practice far-reaching changes in our present typical modes of relation to the living creatures of our natural environment. The responsibilities constitute a significant part of the *demand* aspect of Religion of Nature but I shall argue that they can also contribute profoundly to its other two central aspects of *assurance* and *empowerment*.

Three major developments in the history of the natural sciences have contributed greatly to the need for radical changes in conception and practice regarding the relations of human beings to other forms of life on earth for which I shall plead in this book—changes that are even at present only beginning to filter into our consciousness and to guide our actions. This fact is perhaps not really so surprising, for as environmentalist Andrew C. Revkin reflects, "it is not easy being the first life-form to become both a planet-scale force and—ever so slowly and uncomfortably—aware of that fact."[3] The implications of these developments are articulated and reinforced, in turn, by the orientation and commitments of Religion of Nature.

The three major developments are familiar ones, but I want to bring them and some of their repercussions clearly into view as they relate to the themes of this book. They are as follows:

- The *cosmological* revolution initiated by Nicholas
  Copernicus, endorsed and elaborated by thinkers such
  as Johannes Kepler, Galileo Galilei, and Isaac Newton,
  and carried forward by the stupendous expansion in our
  view of the temporal and the spatial scope of the universe
  by natural scientists of the nineteenth and twentieth
  centuries.

- The *evolutionary* revolution, inaugurated by Charles
  Darwin and Alfred Russel Wallace, and expanded and
  refined by the researches of Gregor Mendel and his
  successors in the field of genetics, the achievements of
  Neo-Darwinism (or the Modern Synthesis), and the rise
  of molecular biology.

- The *ecological* revolution, set in motion by thinkers such
  as Ernst Haeckel, Frederick Clements, Charles Elton,
  and Aldo Leopold, and carried forward by others such as
  Eugene Odum, Barry Commoner, and Rachel Carson.

I want briefly to point out the significance of these three scientific
developments for revisions of the prevalent view of the relations of
humans to the natural order and to living beings within this order
that held sway for millennia in Western culture. This view prevailed
for so long largely because of the influence of pivotal ideas in Western
religion and philosophy that predated both the dawn of the natural
sciences and the three major developments I shall highlight here that
have played central roles in the history of these sciences since the late
sixteenth century.

The Cosmological Revolution

Nicholas Copernicus and the scientists (then called "natural philosophers") who came after him replaced an earth-centered cosmology
with one in which the center is the sun, making the earth but one of
the six then known planets orbiting the sun (Mercury, Venus, Earth,
Mars, Saturn, and Jupiter). As the theologians and philosophers of
the time were well aware, the implications of this shift in thinking for
the place of human beings in the universe were profound. If the earth

as the dwelling place of humans is not the center of things, perhaps humans do not have the central, dominating role in the universe as a whole that had long been assumed. The cozy, relatively simple, three-tiered, band-box universe of prescientific thinking now had to give way to a much more complex and capacious one calling into serious question the ancient cosmological picture in which the sublime starry heavens cupping the earth from above and the raging fiery hell beneath were oriented toward the actions of human beings on the face of the earth, an earth that was assumed to be little more than the divinely appointed transitory stage for the saga of their creation, primordial fall, and final redemption. This earth and all that is in it, including all of its other forms of life, were thought to exist for the sake of human beings, wholly subject to their special needs, interests, duties, and destiny. Nonhuman forms of life constituted a significant part of the *instrumental* goods of the earth, things made good by their subservience to *intrinsic* human goods. But with the de-centering of earth in the cosmos—thought by most thinkers of the time to be confined to the solar system—the way was opened to an eventual de-centering of human beings themselves, since the focus was moving away from a near-exclusive attention to them and their problems and prospects toward increasing scientific interest in more encompassing aspects of the functionings of the earth and solar system.

Isaac Newton was able to unify terrestrial and celestial dynamics, showing that the same fundamental principles govern the solar system as a whole that we find to be operative here on earth. And he was able to put to elegant use his mathematical discovery (along with Gottfried Leibniz) of the calculus, as well as other sophisticated mathematical techniques, in doing so. Galileo Galilei had already announced that the language of physical nature is the language of mathematics, and this idea was increasingly accepted. To think with the language of mathematics was for Galileo to think God's thoughts after Him, to decipher the ingenious plan of the super-intelligent Cosmic Geometer, Designer, and Engineer for the creation and ordering of the world.[4] Johannes Kepler's earlier three precise mathematical laws of planetary motion provided impressive reinforcement for this view.

As a consequence, the universe came to be regarded as a vast mathematical system or mathematically describable mechanism, running smoothly but blindly on its own without the need of any—or at most only occasional, exceedingly rare—divine interventions. There was thus a sense in which not only humans were pushed to the periphery of the inexorable runnings of the cosmic machinery; God himself was made relatively peripheral to that machinery once he had set it in motion. After he had created it, God was no longer required to sustain the universe moment by moment, as had formerly been assumed to be the case. The roles of both God and humans with their respective forms of consciousness and subjectivity were thus in a significant sense marginalized and thrust into the background; the central stage in the new cosmology was given over to the unconscious machinery of nature.

This implicit de-centering of humans was to proceed apace into the nineteenth and twentieth centuries, when both the assumed small age of the cosmos and its limited spatial extent underwent a spectacular expansion. Now, rather than the universe being regarded on the basis of biblical chronology as a few thousand years old, it came to be viewed as nearly *fourteen billion* years old and perhaps as only one of multiple concurrent or successive universes. And the tidy little solar system of earlier scientific thought came to be replaced with a universe believed to have about one-hundred billion galaxies, each containing somewhere around one-hundred billion stars, and no one knows how many planetary systems orbiting at least some of those billions of stars. Such a vision of the cosmos can have the effect of making human history, human cultures, and human affairs seem rather insignificant in the whole scheme of things. The earth itself can appear to be only a fleck of dust in a far-flung, indescribably immense universe.

The seventeenth-century French philosopher René Descartes and others concluded from the emerging scientific world picture of his time that the only exception to the cosmic machinery on earth is human beings, who he thought—in accordance with long-standing philosophical and religious belief—to possess immortal, immaterial souls now seen as somehow residing and operating in machine-like bodies.[5] Thus humans with their conscious souls were contrasted with the whole of nature, *including all of its other life-forms*, as the sole exception to nature's thoroughgoing mathematical and mechanistic character. In one sense, this picture places humans at the margins of nature, as it were, peering at it from the isolated booths of their subjective, qualitative awareness but no longer central to its operations and no longer as easily to be regarded as its principal reason for being.

The other side of this picture is that all nonhuman life-forms are now to be seen as mere objects, devoid of interiority or subjectivity, amenable to manipulation and use in the same manner as inorganic features of the earth such as liquids, metals, and rocks, and in whatever fashions humans might determine or devise. In the utilizations of mere machines, moral considerations do not enter in—except as these utilizations may affect human life and human affairs. Nonhuman life-forms are not deserving of moral considerability or respect for their own sakes, but only, if at all, for the sake of human enterprises, wants, or needs.

So, paradoxically, the earth's de-centering and the implied relegation of humans to the periphery of the solar system and to what was later to be regarded as a universe of countless galaxies also seemed to give humans *carte blanche* for any treatment of nonhuman life-forms human beings decided to inflict upon them.[6] With their capacity for such things as feeling, sensing, imagining, reasoning, and self-awareness, and their assumed possession of immortal souls, humans were viewed as radically distinct from everything else in nature. Nature was envisioned as devoid of quality or inwardness and seen as complex machinery containing nonhuman life-forms as many different kinds of machine.

Thus, once again, though for a different reason, nature was rendered wholly subordinate to the interests, preferences, and needs of human beings. The cosmic *de-centering* of humans had the curious effect for Descartes and other mind-body dualists of a terrestrial *re-centering* of them as the solely conscious overlords of a totally mechanized nature here on earth. They were somehow at the periphery of nature as a whole—the sole, seemingly anomalous exception on earth to earth's and the cosmos's pervasively mechanistic, quantitative character—but were also granted by implication the warrant for a new kind of continuing unbridled dominance, mastery, and control of the natural order on their own planet. These ideas would be called into serious question, however, from two other quarters of a still emerging science: those of the evolutionary revolution of the mid-nineteenth century and the ecological revolution that was to follow.

The Evolutionary Revolution

The quotation from Charles Darwin's 1837 *Notebooks* that I have used as the epigraph for this chapter reveals his exciting conjecture of the "netting together" of humans with all the other life-forms of earth in a long process of evolutionary development from relatively simple primitive forms. It was a mind-boggling conjecture or intimation for his time that he brought to fruition by providing for it carefully reasoned justification and explanation—largely by means of the central notion of "natural selection"—in his books *The Origin of Species* (1859) and *The Descent of Man* (1871). Darwin supported his theory of evolution through natural selection with painstaking references to copious pertinent examples of animal forms, behavior, and relationships, much of this material having been collected on his five-year circumnavigating voyage as a naturalist on the HMS Beagle but supplemented with the results of his lifelong empirical studies.

The upshot of Darwin's work and that of those who continued to think and explore in the evolutionary vein is that humans differ from other life-forms on earth not so much in *kind* as in *degree*, that is, in the possession of distinctive traits defining their species but stemming from a common origin and from common processes governing that origin. These life-forms can now be seen as "kinfolk" to human beings, as fellow adventurers on the long journey of biological evolution, and as variations on basically similar patterns of emergence, structure, behavior, and need. We are all joined together in a shared history and heritage. Instead of being viewed as external lords over nature and warranted masters of its other kinds of life, humans can now be regarded as one spinoff of a mutual evolutionary history reaching into the distant past, one branch of an evolutionary tree with multiple, ever growing branches thrusting in many different directions.

Darwin used this imagery of the tree of evolution with its numerous branchings over an immense past. Some branches have died and fallen off the tree in the form of past extinctions, while new branches have continued to sprout, live, and flourish.[7] This image is not one of linear progression toward any sort of goal—for example, that of the emergence of human beings—but one of undirected, wildly prolific shoots of life bursting out in many different directions, some of them eventually to become dead ends, others giving rise to new branchings of life-forms. And human beings are no longer to be regarded as outliers or aliens set over against internal cosmic and terrestrial processes radically different from their own essential substances or characters. Instead, humans are natural products of those processes and intimate participants in them. Humans are at one with nature, bone of its bone and flesh of its flesh. By implication, the dualistic wall between their inward, subjective, qualitative life and the rest of the world was broken down, meaning that such things as conscious emotion, thought, purpose, and volition could no longer be confined unquestionably to human beings. The way was opened to a new way of envisioning the relations between human and nonhuman forms of life.

This evolutionary narrowing of the gap between humans and other life-forms was furthered and abetted by the nineteenth-century Augustinian friar Gregor Mendel's researches into laws regarding recessive and dominant genetic factors as these affect the inheritance through sexual reproduction of certain traits in pea plants. The significance of Mendel's laws was not recognized until the turn of the twentieth century, when they were independently rediscovered and Mendel's pioneering work newly brought to light. Natural selection as a drive toward evolutionary change could now be complemented with a new and informative perspective on changes occurring in the genetic structures of organisms. This idea lent credibility to the notion that certain random variations in the genetic makeup of some organisms within a species might prove to be more adaptive to the organisms' environments and favor the survival and reproduction of groups of those organisms in which the favorable genetic variations had taken place. Over time, such incremental changes can in this manner lead to the origination of new species. Thus the evolution of a new species can be explained as the result of internal genetic changes guided by the environmental influences of natural selection.

This melding of genetic variations with natural selection, and an accompanying direction of attention to statistical analysis of the inheritance and prevalence of genes within populations of organisms, are at the heart of Neo-Darwinism or the Modern Synthesis. Since the twin factors of genetic variation and natural selection are believed by evolutionary biologists to have been operative in the evolution of hominid and human populations as well as in that of other kinds of populations, the types of population are in this way drawn more tightly together in a common conceptual net.

The last important stage of development in this evolutionary outlook took place with the rise in the mid-twentieth century of molecular biology. This discipline came into its own with the discovery of the structure of the DNA molecule by Francis Crick and James Watson in 1953. The discovery provided dramatic physical evidence of how genetic inheritances take place and also of how genetic mutations can be produced by "mistakes" in transcription and replication from an existing DNA molecule to the formation of another one. This system of genetic reproduction or alteration is now known to be operative in all types of organism on earth. Creatures such as fruit flies, worms, crabs, and humming birds—to say nothing of all species of plants—have genetic structures based on the DNA molecule. And through detailed analyses of their respective genotypes, animals such as chimpanzees can now be shown to share a large percentage (95%–99%) of their DNA makeup with humans, a result that shows their close evolutionary kinship to humans. There are still important differences in the last two species' overall genetic functionings, including which and when specific genes are turned on or off for members of the two species' developmental processes, but the close similarity of genotypes remains striking. It gives further convincing indication of a joint evolutionary descent of humans and other species. Veterinarian and animal ethicist Michael W. Fox provides a good summary of the revolutionary impact of evolutionary theory so far as the concept of humanity and its place in nature are concerned when he says of us humans: "Our bodies contain the mineral elements of primordial rocks; our very cells share the same historically evolved components as those of grasses and trees; our brains contain the basic neural core of reptile, bird, and fellow mammal."[8] We are not set apart from nature but are one with it. We depend critically upon it at every turn, and it suffuses every aspect of our being.

The Ecological Revolution

The ecological revolution takes its name from the Greek word *oikos*, which means house, household, domicile, or by extension a place of common dwelling. As historian Donald Worster points out in his excellent, highly detailed history of the origination and development of ecology as a branch of the natural sciences, the term *Oecologie* was coined in 1866 by Ernst Haeckel, a leading German disciple of Darwin. Haeckel conceived of this new type of science as the study of specific groups of organisms of many different types dwelling intimately together in a kind of household or family, in typical family relations of conflict as well as mutual dependency, and with close relations to their inorganic environments.[9] Such organisms and their external environments are thus to be seen as complex, intricately inter-active *systems*, not as mere aggregations of independent units of study.

Just as Darwin had earlier defended the notion that all organisms are netted together through *time* by their shared evolutionary origins, Haeckel was now arguing that they are also bound closely together by their relations in *space*, that is, by their here-and-now dynamic patterns of intimate cooperation and competition. Organisms do not live in self-sufficient independence and are not to be studied as though they do so or *could* do so. Instead, if organisms are to be fully understood, they need to be studied together, as parts of an interactive, interdependent family or household of creatures.

An important version of this idea was vigorously propounded by Frederick Clements, a Nebraska native whose most influential book *Plant Succession: An Analysis of the Development of Vegetation*, appeared in 1916. Clements stressed the dynamic and interdependent character of ecological communities and even went so far as to view these communities as whole organisms or super-organisms that function as such in their own right. He also contended that particular types of biological communities, despite their initial volatility, will over time reach a characteristic state of general stability, order, and balance that he characterized as a climax system. Once having reached this stage, the type of ecological community may be disrupted by external influences, principally by changes in the weather, but it will always tend back toward the equilibrium of its climax character.

The community will do so, Clements argued, in much the same way as an individual organism undergoes typical stages of change and development in progressing toward its mature state. Clements believed that since mature communities have this organismic, holistic, predictable character, they can be subjected to rigorous scientific analysis and explanation. The status of ecology as a natural science was enhanced by this idea, even though the notion of a natural and virtually inevitable terminal balance or stability of such systems was to be brought into serious dispute by later thinkers. The precise character and boundaries—if any—of an alleged ecological community or ecosystem also turned out to be not nearly as easily determined or agreed upon as Clements had believed.

A key figure in the development of ecological ideas was the Cambridge zoologist Charles Elton, whose first major work, *Animal Ecology*, was published in 1927. In his "account of the natural economy as a simplified economy," Worster writes, "twentieth-century ecology found its single most important paradigm."[10] Elton, in conceiving of ecological systems as a type of "economy," sought to analyze their existing forms and functions (rather than, as with Clements, their alleged processes of succession and climax) as the ways their members make use of the total amount of sources of food available to them within their environments. Two influential concepts emerging from his thinking along these lines are those of *food chains* and ecological *niches*. Elton reasoned that organisms within an ecosystem are linked together by their dependence on acquiring and eating types of food suited to and necessary for their particular modes of life and survival, and also by the lower and more numerous elements of the food chain—for example, krill, plants, and insects—providing food for the less numerous ones higher up in the chain—for example, whales, deer, and bats.[11] In participating in this food chain, each kind of organism occupies its own occupational niche within the environment, its own specific way of making its living. No two species can have the same niche in a single ecological community, according to Elton; all others are excluded from a niche by a particular species' competitive success in gaining it. The two key ideas of food chains and ecological niches, and Elton's model of ecosystems as integrated economies, lent itself to the view—brought into prominence by thinkers such as the Oxford botanist A. G. Tansley, of ecosystems as various ways of making use of the energy of the sun, starting with the photosynthesis of plants, algae, and cyanobacteria.[12]

Worster notes in passing that Elton viewed humans as outsiders, "not to be confused with the natural economic system and its workings."[13] The notion that humans can be excluded from the natural workings of ecosystems, that they are not natural participants in ecological relations, is an old one, as we have seen. It was to be contested in later ecological thinking, although it continued well into the twentieth century under the moniker, attitudes, and practices of *conservation*. The notion is suggestive of the old assumption that human beings are somehow external to nature and the sole earthly exceptions to natural processes. They stand outside nature and look at it from the outside rather than being an integral part of it and having to view it from within. One ecologist who was to take issue with this persistent notion, what many ecologists and other thinkers now regard as a dangerous and destructive delusion, was Aldo Leopold.

However, Leopold was, in the early 1930s, greatly influenced by the main thrust of Elton's ecological thinking.[14]

Like Clements, Leopold was an American born in the Midwest. He emphasized two basic ideas in his widely read *Sand County Almanac*, published in 1949 shortly after his death. One is the radical interdependence of plants and animals in their natural environments; and the other is the notion that human beings, as one type of animal, are constitutive, dependent, and accountable members of those environments. In other words, humans are not exceptions to ecological principles but are tightly bound by them, and they are as much intimate parts of ecological relations as are all other types of organism. Leopold pled in this book and in the thought and activity of his later years for a replacement of the conventional anthropocentric orientation of an earlier conservationist movement, for which he himself had once been a strong advocate, with an outlook explicitly centered on nature, one in which humans are recognized to have a subordinate and participatory rather than a dominant and controlling role. He wrote that what he called a *land ethic* "changes the role of *Homo sapiens* from conqueror of the land-community to plain member and citizen of it. It implies respect for his fellow-members, and also respect for the community as such."[15]

Leopold acknowledged that humans are entitled, as are all species, to make appropriate use of the resources of nature, but they are not entitled to endanger or despoil aspects of nature at will, simply to satisfy their own idiosyncratic demands. In fact, to the extent that they insist on doing the latter, they threaten not only the health and viability of nonhuman life-forms but their own well-being as a species critically dependent on those life-forms and the integrity of their complexly entangled patterns of relationship with one another and with their inorganic environments. Leopold's version of the ecological revolution thus has the effect—along with the cosmological and evolutionary revolutions—of shifting the spotlight away from humans and focusing it on the whole of nature of which they are only a part, but a potentially reckless and destructive part.

An ecologist who took a holistic approach to the flora and fauna of earth and their relations to the nonliving environment was the North Carolinian Eugene Odum. He was particularly interested in ecosystems, which he regarded as the basic functional unit in ecology. His most influential book is a textbook entitled *Fundamentals of Ecology*, first published in 1953, going through many subsequent editions, and translated into many languages. Odum characterized an ecosystem as "any unit that includes all of the organisms . . . in a given area interacting with the physical environment so that a flow of energy leads to clearly defined trophic structure, biotic diversity, and material cycles (i.e., exchange of materials between living and nonliving parts) within the system."[16] He held a view reminiscent in at least one way of Clement's concept of climax systems, namely, that ecosystems in their very nature had already achieved, were well on their way to achieving, or were struggling to re-achieve a state of equilibrium he termed *homeostasis*.

An ecosystem is thus a complex of interdependent organisms, interlocked with the conditions of a particular sort of nonliving environment, which exhibits and is capable of maintaining a distinctive identity, balance, and character over long periods of time. It and its relations to other ecosystems should, according to Odum, be the principal focus of ecological science, a focus amenable to rigorous analysis and prediction. Unfortunately, the notion has turned out, to a significant extent, to be rather indistinct and vague when subjected to close empirical examination. That is to say, what precisely is to count as a particular ecosystem has in many cases been found to be elusive and not at all easy to determine. Nevertheless, the concept of an ecosystem and the need for a holistic, nonreductive, systems approach it implies has played and continues to play a significant role in ecological thought, and it has made a powerful impression on the popular mind.

Odum gave special attention throughout his life to the place of humans in nature and their relations to the ecosystems of the earth. He wanted humans to accept the responsibility of doing what they can to keep what he called "Space-Ship Earth" in as natural a state as possible, that is, to preserve the natural balance and equilibrium of the earth's complexly entwined ecosystems. Far from being separate from nature, humans are integral parts of it, both crucially depending upon and also crucially affecting its health and well-being. In viewing earth as nothing more than a storehouse of external resources for human exploitation and use, humans are in danger, Odum persistently argued, of destroying their own life-support system on Space-Ship Earth. Thinking and arguing in this way, Odum made a marked contribution to reformist environmental movements and environmental ethics.

Barry Commoner and Rachel Carson are two examples of other scientists who had an important effect on public consciousness and environmental politics. Commoner called attention to the destructive effects of nitrate-based chemical fertilizers on the public's water supply and on the body's ability to transport oxygen in the blood. He also vividly described the rank pollution of Lake Erie from the phosphates in household detergents. These were for him indications of how destructive such human practices could be when guided by nothing more than a relentless pursuit of profits. Carson's disturbing book *The Silent Spring*, published in 1962, was highly effective in bringing public attention to the destructive effects on organisms in the natural environment of the widespread use of the herbicide DDT. The message of her book was not only that humans are endangering the lives of other species by their reckless use of materials that can accumulate in the tissues of plants and animals and even alter their germ cells and reproductive capacity, but that humans are in this way mounting serious threats to their own lives and to their survival as a species in the process.

In other words, humans are part of ecosystems or patterns of ecological dependency. Human policies and practices that have deleterious effects on ecosystems will also have inevitable and perhaps in some cases irreversible similar effects on human lives. In highlighting such boomerang effects, Commoner and Carson—along with many others who issued similar warnings in the second half of the twentieth century and on into the twenty-first—showed how integral to ecological relations human beings are, and how little able they are to stand apart from the consequences of these relations in either the short or the long run.

Worster takes careful notice of the fact that ecology is still a young science and that its history is one of marked disagreements among ecologists about even some of its most basic concepts and contentions. For example, there are mechanists and organicists among them, the former seeking to treat ecology as a branch of physics and the latter arguing for emergent properties in organisms and their relationships that must be analyzed and explained in their own terms and in their own right. There are those who stress the general integrity and stability of ecosystems and those who emphasize their fluidity, vagueness, overlappings of supposed boundaries, and constant disturbances, even to the extent of doubting the meaning or usefulness of the very idea of distinctive ecosystems. There are individualists who put emphasis on the characteristics and behaviors of particular organisms and holists who focus on whole systems and their patterns of interrelation. There are strict causal determinists and other ecologists who stress the role of chance in ecological processes. Finally, there are those who give a large place to chaos theory, complexity theory, and non-linear dynamics in their studies of ecological issues, and others who do not.

Worster shrewdly remarks that ecologists continue to be persons of faith, convinced that there must be a large degree of rational order underlying the daunting volatility and complexity of ecological systems and relations. Their continuing task is to uncover it, formulate it, and test it scientifically.[17] Seasoned botanist Richard Ward states in a personal note, however, that he is "doubtful that there will ever be any over-arching, 'unified theory' for ecology—the diversity, complexity, instability, uncertainty, etc. of nature, living and non-living, are together too great for other than restricted theories." The spirit of his statement is echoed by Kuang-ming Wu in his evocative book on the Daoist text *Chaung Tzu*. "Anything that is observable, conscious, and objective," Wu writes, "is static, abstract, and therefore an ossification. Life is, in contrast, always flowing, growing and self transforming; in a word, life is alive or nothing. And anything alive is difficult to classify accurately into the pigeon holes of abstraction and generalization."[18]

Ward observes in another personal note that that the probability of finding supposed ecosystems with precisely definable boundaries is extremely low at best. He prefers to speak of *gradients* of populations of plants in relation to particular locales and of *continua* or subtle mixings of such gradients from locale to locale rather than assuming or hoping to discover sharp distinctions among the gradients.

Two things do seem to be common to all of the variations in ecological thinking at present, and they are of primary importance for my own ruminations in this book. They are (1) that organisms of various types are radically entwined with and dependent upon one another for their continual flourishing and survival as they make common if varied use of the energy of the sun; and (2) that human beings are among the creatures of nature so inexorably entwined and dependent. The precise details of this picture remain elusive and difficult to determine, and we will perhaps never have a completely satisfactory unitary way of conceiving them. But the picture itself holds true. Humans have not only emerged from natural processes; they remain subject to them and responsible to them in fundamental ways that none of their technological and cultural achievements give them ability or license to avoid or annul.

It is true that, as Paul Colinvaux indicates, humans are not confined to a particular ecological niche as are other biological species in their natural states. Instead, humans have become, in the last nine thousand years, able "to change their niche at will." They have done so by learning to domesticate and herd animals instead of hunting them and by inventing agriculture.

> Herding increased our food resource, because it denied other predators a chance at the game we had corralled; it let us kill prime animals when we wanted them, and it let us waste less calories in the inefficient process of hunting. Agriculture increased our food supply still more, because with it went a plant diet that would let us move down the Eltonian pyramids of our lands one whole trophic level. . . . Herding and agriculture entailed the adoption of entirely new niches. For the first time an animal had adopted a new niche without speciating. It was the most momentous event in the history of life.[19]

But with this special ability comes the foolish temptation to view ourselves as somehow exempt from the larger contexts and relations of nature.

Succumbing to that temptation means failure to recognize the special responsibility that accompanies the special gift. Our ability to alter nature to a significant degree by our domestication and herding of animals, our increasingly sophisticated agricultural practices, and other highly developed technological discoveries, inventions, and cultural creations—to say nothing of our exponentially burgeoning human population—also allow us to introduce radical, unprecedented instabilities into aspects of nature; to interfere with its natural checks and balances; to threaten the very existence of many of its diverse species of organism; to pollute and despoil its land, oceans, and air; perhaps to bring about sudden phase transitions or major tipping points in its temperatures and patterns of climate; and the like.

The Lesson of the Three Scientific Revolutions

When our crucial dependence on the nonhuman aspects of nature is forgotten or arrogantly ignored, we humans can wreak considerable damage and ruin not only on those aspects of nature but also on ourselves as part of the age-old systematic interconnections of all natural beings. "What we call the environmental movement of the post-World War Two era," Worster remarks, "has been essentially a reawakening to the realization that we must depend on other forms of life to survive; we have no other options. Progress has not made our condition different in this respect from that of our remotest ancestors."[20] This is a lesson of the ecological revolution that we neglect at our peril. Neglect of it would also be a callous forfeiture of the grave and urgent responsibility we owe to the whole community of natural beings to which we are privileged to belong. The lesson of human beings' cosmological, evolutionary, and ecological decentering as but one among myriad, ever-evolving, mutually dependent creatures of nature is a hard one to learn after so many centuries of sharply separating ourselves from the whole of the natural order and assuming that we have the right to master and manipulate it solely for our own benefit. But discoveries of the natural sciences impel us to take this lesson seriously to heart. The lesson is also drummed into us today by such fields of thought and action as philosophy of nature, environmental ethics, animal ethics, and religious naturalism (including Religion of Nature). And it is now being taken into account by increasing numbers of adherents of the major world religions.[21]

So far in this book, I have sought to highlight the demand aspect of Religion of Nature as that grows out of and is made explicit in the three scientific revolutions I have brought under discussion. The discussion up to this point has admittedly been quite general. But I shall endeavor to make this aspect more specific and detailed in subsequent chapters, particularly as it relates to our attitude toward and treatment of nonhuman forms of life. In addition, I shall seek to draw out the other two central dimensions of Religion of Nature already mentioned, namely, the dimensions of assurance and empowerment, and show how these dimensions as well are closely connected with the overall outlook on and orientation to nature I am developing here and calling the Thou of Nature.

2

Inwardness and Awareness in Nature

Behaviorism in psychology and reductionism in biology were so dominant from roughly the 1920s to the 1960s that scientists were reluctant even to consider the possibility that there was such a thing as animal cognition, let alone animal consciousness.

—Donald Griffin[1]

Introduction

Zoologist Donald Griffin devotes the article from which the epigraph for this chapter is taken to a refutation of the notion that consciousness is the exclusive trait of human beings rather than having an important role in the lives of many nonhuman animals. He concludes the article by saying, "Most of Darwin's basic ideas about evolution are now generally accepted by scientists, but the notion that there has been evolutionary continuity with respect to conscious experiences is still strongly resisted. Overcoming this resistance may be the final crowning chapter of the Darwinian revolution."[2] We have here yet another important implication of the evolutionary revolution discussed in the previous chapter, the idea that there has been a continuity of development throughout the history of biological revolution that has permitted a gradually increasing capacity for sentient awareness and cognitive capability in various forms of life and that blossomed finally into the fullness of consciousness and self-awareness possessed by human beings. The human mode of consciousness exhibits at best, therefore, the outcome of a gradually emerging difference of degree when compared with modes of awareness characteristic of many other organisms, not a radical difference of kind. The purpose of this chapter is to defend Griffin's claim and to draw out some of its consequences for Religion of Nature.

The title of this book, *The Thou of Nature*, is not intended to imply any sort of pantheistic, panentheistic, or animistic conception of nature and our relations as human beings to nonhuman aspects of nature. It is intended rather to call attention to the inward, first-hand, and thus "thou" character of forms of life and to plead for our becoming aware of both the possibility and the urgent need to adopt the stance of an I-thou relationship with living beings in the natural world. This need is especially urgent as it pertains to our relations with animals capable of suffering and pain as well as experiencing palpable exuberance and joy in the course of their lives. For too long we in the West and in other parts of the world have tended to regard nonhuman life-forms solely or primarily as objects of external study, manipulation, use, or entertainment, and for too long we have taken insufficient notice of the fact of their inwardness—the internality of their actions and ways in which they go about relating to, altering, and affecting, as well as being affected by, their natural environments.

Our dominant scientific model for understanding other living beings has long been the impersonal one of the machine. We have regarded organisms as complexes of mechanistic processes and relations that can, at least in principle, be understood by purely objective modes of analysis and synthesis, disassembly and reassembly. We have tended uncritically to assume that adequate understanding of these organisms requires that we examine, explain, and conceive them and their functions in exclusively external, mechanistic, quantifiable ways. Scientific objectivity and the reliability and testability of its theories, we have told ourselves, require this approach. Whatever empathetic, emotional, or qualitative experiences we might have in relation to life-forms other than our own have been assumed by many past scientists to have little or no cognitive significance and next to zero scientific importance. In countering this way of thinking, biologist Marc Bekoff observes that "we need much more than traditional science—science that is not socially responsible, science that is autonomous and authoritarian, science that fragments the universe and disembodies and alienates humans and other animals—to make headway into understanding other animals and the world at large."[3] We need also to draw upon the resources of areas of thought other than the natural sciences such as those of the social sciences, the arts, history, philosophy, and religion as we seek to understand the complexity and range of our resemblances and relations to life-forms other than ourselves.

In the process of seeking to comprehend living beings exclusively from the outside we have tended to lose sight of the inwardness that is characteristic of all life, even in its most primitive forms, and that becomes ever more sophisticated, subtle, and sensitive in the experiences of neurologically complex types of living beings such as birds, fish, reptiles, and mammals as they find ways to flourish within their natural environments. This inwardness of life is reflected in our own relatively high level of—but by no means exclusive possession of—conscious feeling, cognitive awareness, and intentional action. When it comes to subjectivity, the difference between us and other life-forms is, as I noted earlier, one of degree, not of categorical distinction. In other words, we are far from being the only creatures on earth with genuine inwardness, subjective awareness, or truly first-hand thouness or sentience. I shall explain why we must recognize the truth of this claim and why we should incorporate into our lives the incontrovertible metaphysical, moral, and (as I shall eventually show) religious implications of its being true.

In what follows I first defend the thesis that nature is an interconnected system of thous reaching far beyond human thous, meaning that an I-thou relation with much of nature is not only conceivable but morally compelling. I note the pragmatic value and importance to evolutionary life-forms of increasing levels of internal awareness as they develop ways of constituting, adapting to, and transforming their environments. I also seek to show that acknowledging the pervasive inwardness of all living beings is a matter of urgent practical importance for us humans as well, and not merely a theoretical one of "neutral, discoverable fact."[4] This is so both because this acknowledgment bears in countless ways on how we conduct our lives in their relation to the nonhuman parts of nature and because it bears profoundly on our own nature and destiny as natural beings.

Inwardness of Life and Inwardness of Mind

In making a case for the inwardness or *thou* character of all forms of life, I follow the analysis of Evan Thompson in his insightful and appropriately entitled book *Mind in Life*.[5] Thompson argues that there are two minimal conditions for anything being properly identified as a living system: *autopoiesis* (or self-making) and *cognition* (or sense-making). An autopoietic system is one that actively produces and maintains from within itself and by means of its own internal resources (hence the term *inwardness*) a semipermeable boundary between itself and what lies outside itself. This boundary separates it from the world and identifies its distinctive character as something separate from the world but also enables it to interact with the world and to define or constitute for itself what counts as its particular environment, milieu, or lived world.

Such a self-sustaining system is dynamic rather than static, striving continuously to respond to and adapt itself to changes in its external environment, including changes brought about by its movements within that environment. Its adaptiveness is not merely passive because it includes alterations the ongoing activity of the life system is capable of producing in its environment. Thus it both dynamically affects, as well as being affected by, its environment. Honey bees feed on and are nourished by the nectar of flowers, and in so doing they carry pollen from plant to plant, fertilizing the plants in the process and helping thereby to maintain the plants' presence in the environment. Seeds falling onto the rock face of a hillside can produce plants (including trees) whose root-thrusts and agitations are capable of grinding the rocks into soil and dissolving and drawing upon the nutrients in that soil as the plants develop. Beavers convert running streams into still ponds with their industrious dam building, and they construct lodges there with underwater entrances that protect them and their progeny from predators. Other species are able to flourish in the ponds. Even a simple eukaryotic cell transports molecules and energy from its external environment through its cell wall into its interior and is thus able to replenish and maintain the biochemical components and structures of its cellular boundary and interior. And on it goes.

This responsive and proactive adaptiveness is what amounts for Thompson to the cognitive or sense-making character of a living system. This capability is another indication of the inwardness of all life-forms. They make sense out of their environments by relating to them in a manner necessary for maintaining their lives and enhancing their well-being. This process includes the selection and ingestion of nutrients from the environment and the discharge of wastes into the environment. Thompson gives reasons for concluding that viruses, crystals, mitochondria, autocatalytic sets of molecules, and replicative molecules such as DNA and RNA are not alive, but that bacteria and amoebae are.[6] The essential inwardness of life is characteristic, therefore, of a large portion of nature. If the term *inwardness* seems vague, exaggerated, or mysterious in its twin references to autopoiesis and cognition, I respond that it calls appropriate attention to the distinctive character and pronounced mystery of life itself.

In personal correspondence, philosopher and theologian David Conner objects that *cognition* is the wrong term for Thompson to use concerning this function. The term implies, in Conner's view, "an unnecessary and . . . obfuscating reliance on the notion of consciousness." A response to this objection and one well worth considering is that of ecological writer Carl Safina: "Bubble-wrapped within our estrangement from our extended family, we fail to appreciate other animals' competencies. *We withhold recognition of their cognitive abilities.* Blinded to stark evidence of our relatedness to other beings, we heap praise on ourselves for supposedly 'unique' abilities, whose origins are so plain in birds and bees"[7] In other words, we should be careful not to underestimate or peremptorily dismiss the possibility of cognition, even if often only in minimal forms, in beings other than ourselves. We should try to take fully into account the notable similarities in capability and behavior between us and them. Thompson's terminology and outlook help to point us in that direction.

If someone objects on semantic grounds, as Conner does, to use of the term *cognition* in this connection, then that person can opt for Thompson's alternative to it, namely, *sense-making*. Both terms are attempts to call attention to the remarkable capability of life-forms to identify, adapt to, and in many cases alter their environments by actively drawing upon resources within themselves. There is no compelling reason to restrict such terms to the actions and capabilities of human beings, with their specific levels of consciousness and distinctive modes of adaptation, acculturation, intelligence, and their linguistic facility. The two terms can function as useful reminders of our many close similarities to, and not just differences from, other life-forms on earth. I shall continue to use the term *cognition* with the larger meaning in mind but with the caveat that it be interpreted as Thompson interprets it.

Thompson asserts that the autopoietic and cognitive character of living beings does not require, although it provides the necessary basis for, other features descriptive of many forms of life. The features are sentience, intentionality, and purpose. He defines *sentience* as "the feeling of being alive and exercising effort in movement" and as "a kind of primitively self-aware liveliness or animation of the body" of an organism.[8] *Intentionality* is an organism's ability to envision and construct, however basically, its world, and to act with some degree of awareness in reference to it. *Purpose* is striving with some level of conscious awareness toward ends or goals implicit in this acting. The immanent striving or *conatus* of all life-forms for their own self-preservation lies behind such conscious striving. Not all forms of life are consciously aware in these three respects—*all three of which* I include in the meaning of the term *sentience*, in contrast to Thompson's more restricted usage of that term. But all forms of life have the crucial traits of autopoiesis and cognition (as defined by Thompson) that underlie and make possible conscious awareness in its various stages of evolutionary development among living beings.

Accordingly, Thompson suggests, the gap to be studied by scientists, philosophers, and others should no longer be conceived as yawning dualistically or in stark Cartesian fashion between body and mind but as being between two types of bodies—a body-body gap. The two types exhibit a shared ontology, namely, that of bodily organisms *lacking* and of bodily organisms *possessing* some degree of conscious awareness—the latter now being understood as gradually building, through evolutionary processes, on potentialities already present in the essential inwardness of the former.[9] Thus the so-called gap can be more accurately perceived as a *continuum* or at least as relatively short jumps from earlier to later forms of organic beings.

Consciousness, Thompson muses, "would seem to require (in ways we do not yet fully understand) the reflexive elaboration and interpretation of life processes provided by the nervous system" and should be viewed as situated "in relation to dynamic, unconscious processes of life regulation."[10] These non-conscious processes entail, in their turn, a dynamic, self-regulating, self-sustaining, reciprocal, and persistent relation of inwardness and outwardness, a relation distinctive to all forms of life. In other words, *were there no inwardness, there would be no life.* The inwardness of mind, in its turn, rests upon the inwardness of life.

To approach life from a purely or even primarily external perspective is to run the risk of leaving out of account and failing to comprehend what is most basic and essential to it. The mystery of inwardness is not confined to us humans; it reaches deeply into nature and characterizes all forms of life. The relatively recent scientific investigations into autopoiesis and into what Thompson describes as organic cognition or sense-making have helped to make this fact clear. The moral of this story is that what may start out as external, third-hand scientific approaches to the phenomenon of life can end up having to give due recognition to its essentially internal, first-hand character.

An extremely important step toward recognizing the presence of mentality and consciousness in other life-forms is acknowledging, as Thompson does, the inwardness of life itself. There is no unbridgeable gap between the "outwardness" of non-living matter, therefore, and the inwardness of mind because mental functioning, like life itself, can be conceived as a capability of highly structured organic *bodies* acquired through a long process of biological evolution. But this is only a first step. In the next section I want to present a number of other considerations that lead to the conclusion that what Thompson calls sentience, intentionality, and purpose—and thus the rudimentary but most telling traits of mind and consciousness, the conceptions of which, as I indicated earlier, I include under the common term *sentience*—are, far from being confined to us humans, commonplace throughout nature. In doing so, I continue to prepare a case for the major conclusion of this book, which is that many life-forms in nature are richly deserving of carefully nurtured, resolutely practiced moral considerability and religious regard.

Mind and Consciousness in Nature

In addition to Thompson's observations about the inwardness of life and its connection with and anticipation of the inwardness of mind, there are five other considerations that give support to the idea that mind and consciousness are rampant in nature and by no means confined to human beings. They are the continuity of evolutionary development; the evolutionary advantage or survival value of consciousness; the similarities of neurological structure between human and many nonhuman forms of life that imply similarities of function; multiple behavioral indications; and a burden of proof when it comes to treatment of nonhuman life-forms. I want briefly to examine each of these considerations in turn and in this way sum up what I regard as convincing reasons for ascribing consciousness, in at least some degree, to a large number of living beings.

1. *The continuity of evolutionary development*. This consideration is stated, as we saw at the beginning of this chapter, by Griffin when he speaks of resistance among some scientists to the clear implication of the conception of evolutionary continuity that there should be no abrupt, unprecedented, inexplicable eruption of consciousness only in human organisms. New types of organism do come into being in Darwin's story of evolution, and with them new traits, functions, and capacities, but they do so on the basis of older types of organism and older modes of life. Here there are no *de novo*, wholly unprecedented, absolute changes. All changes are *transformations* of something already there, something that has previously evolved.

In other words, in the evolutionary way of thinking continuity and novelty go necessarily together. The latter is not possible without having a large part of its basis, condition, or precedence in the former. Something as distinctive as consciousness could not have sprung suddenly and fully into being only in humans; it must have been slowly and steadily built up to and anticipated by earlier stages of evolutionary development. This being the case, we would expect to find ample evidences of its presence in other forms of life. Absence of such evidences would call the theory of evolution itself into serious question, at least insofar as it applies to and includes human beings, and thus make implausible if not incredible Darwin's notion of "the descent of man" from earlier stages of evolutionary development in nature.

2. *The evolutionary advantage or survival value of consciousness*. Why has consciousness evolved out of the seedbed of the unconscious (but nevertheless inward) autopoietic and cognitive processes characteristic of all forms of life? The answer, we can assume, is that consciousness in whatever degree has practical use and importance for organisms by providing new ways of exploring and exploiting aspects of their respective natural environments. Once endowed with consciousness, organisms can remember, avoid, anticipate, choose, and

plan in ways that unconscious organisms cannot. Their actions become more resilient and varied, contextual and efficient, and their strategies and resources for survival are made more subtle, inventive, and complex. Outcomes of available courses of action can be mentally recalled and weighed rather than having to be repeatedly dealt with in a purely instinctual or repetitive trial-and-error manner. Animal behavior research scientist Jonathan Balcombe observes that the evolution of consciousness and its presence in many life-forms should not come as a surprise to anyone. "Once creatures began to move about it was, arguably, only a matter of time before consciousness followed. Awareness is enormously adaptive. It enables the organism to make sound choices. In a complex, changing world, that's very useful."[11]

I should note, however, that consciousness as such does not require *self*-consciousness. That arises at further stages of evolution. Philosopher of mind Ned Block rightly notes that "phenomenal consciousness . . . is something we share with many animals." It consists of things like experiencing a headache, tasting chocolate, or seeing red. Phenomenal consciousness as Block describes it is distinct from clear and focused awareness of oneself, which is relatively rare among types of organism and seems to be most pronounced in humans.[12] Experiments have shown that great apes, dolphins, and elephants can pass the test of mirror self-recognition. When a conspicuous mark is placed on the forehead of a great ape, for example, and a mirror is held up to the ape, the experimenter notes whether or not it touches the mark on its forehead or tries to remove it. If it does so, the experimenter concludes that the ape is self-aware. Great apes have passed the test.

The fact that magpies can also pass this test reveals, as Balcombe asserts, that "the evolution of self-awareness" has taken place "independently in a separate lineage." Birds lack the convoluted neocortex of animal brains and have instead in their evolution "undergone proliferation of the paleocortex, which in mammals is not responsible for cognition."[13] The independent line of development of the capacity of self-awareness shows that evolution has led through separate paths to a similar end, and this fact, in turn, suggests the importance of this and other more common cognitive capacities and modes of awareness among nonhuman life-forms as significant contributors to evolutionary adaptation and survival.

3. *Similarities of neurological structure imply similarities of mental functioning*. Thompson suggests, as we saw above, that consciousness

requires some sort of nervous system, but this observation raises the issue of what can count as a nervous system. Bekoff comments that "in humans the amygdala and hypothalamus are important in emotional experiences and that they are mediated by neurotransmitters such as dopamine, serotonin and, oxytocin. We also know that many animals, especially mammals, share with humans the same neurological structures and chemicals." He hastens to add, "Of course, this does not necessarily mean animals share our feelings, but careful observation of individuals during social encounters suggests that at least some of them do."[14]

Despite Bekoff's cautionary tone, such marked similarity of structure does seem to warrant belief in similarity of function and outcome, and thus some significant amount of conscious, first-hand, qualitative experience (that is, experiences of color, sound, tactile sensation, taste, odor, pleasure, pain, fear, anger, and the like) among animals with these particular neurological components. We can adopt as a general rule, then, the idea that the more similarity there is between our complex neurological structures and those of other organisms, the more likely it becomes that they will exhibit some level of Thompson's key conceptions of sentience, intentionality, and purpose and have first-hand experiences similar in at least some respects to our own. We admittedly cannot be certain that this is the case, but as we ascend the scales of similarity and complexity of neurological structure and chemical activity the probabilities weigh rather heavily in the rule's favor. It is entirely safe to assume, as does biologist and neuroscientist Terrence W. Deacon, "that animals with very small brains (such as gnats) can have only the dimmest if any conscious experience, while large-brained animals are quite capable of intense subjective experiences and likely suffer as much as would a person if injured."[15]

But what about dissimilarities such as the one noted earlier between magpies and humans? We saw that magpies exhibit self-awareness but that they have only a paleocortex and not the neocortex that is such a prominent feature of human brains. However, magpies do share with humans and many other life-forms the possession of a paleocortex, showing that the neurological structures do not have to be similar in all respects in order to allow for consciousness in some degree, and in this case, even awareness of self. The basic question we need to ask is why there should be such marked similarities of structure if there is no related similarity of function, utility, and need among various life-forms.

If conscious awareness, at least in some degree, has the evolutionary survival value I associated with it above, and there is undeniable similarity of structure in the neurological systems of many organic species, would it not follow that the end of the first is subserved by the second as its means? Would it make sense to think that these widespread common structures give rise to and support consciousness in the human species alone? Such an abrupt break in evolutionary continuity is hardly credible. So the three considerations of evolutionary continuity, the great utility of consciousness as a means to flourishing and survival, and the similarities of neurological structures (and chemicals) combine and mutually support one another as convincing support for the thesis that consciousness, in minimal or more elaborate forms of what Thompson defines as sentience, intentionality, and purpose (the conceptions of which I define more generally and collectively as sentience), is characteristic of many species of life other than the human species. It is important to note, as Griffin does, that the conscious experience of members of other species "need not be identical to human conscious experience; indeed, it is likely to differ substantially in accordance with the animal's way of life, its sensory capabilities, and its capacity for learning, memory, and anticipation."[16] Consciousness can come in many different forms and still be consciousness.

4. *Behavioral evidences of consciousness.* One of the best evidences of consciousness in nonhuman life-forms is instances or patterns of behavior that indicate experiences of emotion. Balcombe speaks convincingly, I think, when he says that "emotions likely evolved simultaneously with consciousness, for the two serve each other and require a similar leap in mental complexity." And he notes that telling behavioral indications of fear are commonplace among vertebrate animals in threatening situations. Most of them "respond to signs of danger in ways consistent with an experience of fear. They may cringe, flee, freeze, or assume a threatening posture."[17] Such behaviors are of course quite consistent with our own behaviors in threatening situations, and we can reasonably conclude that they are accompanied in animals as in us by something similar to our own direct experiences of wariness, defensiveness, and dread. In a chapter on the evidences

of emotion among nonhuman animals, Balcombe describes modes of behavior among them that can plausibly be interpreted to express such first-hand feelings, or simulacra of them, as gratitude, anxiety, optimism, pessimism, boredom, stress, depression, enjoyment, compassion, sadness, regret, trauma, friendship, mourning, grief, and preference. The examples he discusses of animal behaviors indicating such feelings include chimpanzees, monkeys, starlings, parrots, dogs, elephants, zebras, rats, and mice.

Primatologist Frans De Waal provides us with a striking example of frustration and expectation in the behavior of a monkey. He writes,

> [W]e know that a monkey who has learned to find a banana hidden in a particular location will act nonplussed if the banana has been secretly replaced by a mere leaf of lettuce. At first she will leave the leaf of lettuce untouched, look around, and inspect the location over and over. She may even turn to the experimenter and shriek at him. Only after a long delay will she "content" herself with the lettuce. How to explain such behavior except as the product of a mismatch between reality and expectation?[18]

Expectation is of course a mental phenomenon as is frustration, and the behavior of the monkey gives every indication of these states being consciously experienced by the monkey. Only a strong antecedent bias against the possibility of consciousness in nonhuman animals would absolutely preclude our natural tendency and willingness to attribute some degree of consciousness to the monkey's observed behavior. In so doing, we are not guilty of flagrant anthropomorphism; we are simply drawing a reasonable conclusion. Outward behavior can give convincing evidence of an inward phenomenon.

If it be objected that such an inference is *unscientific* since science deals only with what can be objectively observed, then the objector is insisting on a significant limitation of what he or she describes as science, showing that, as described, it cannot be deemed competent to provide adequate interpretations or explanations of important aspects of nonhuman forms of life. A too hasty and uncritical assimilation of particular animal behaviors with similar human ones and their accompanying mental states is admittedly to be avoided. But equally to be avoided is an adamant refusal to allow for any kind of inference from objective behaviors to subjective experiences in animals. When such inferences are allowed, a strong case can be made for the reality of animal consciousness, at least in some form and in some degree.

A further objection might be that the only way we can be sure that a human being is undergoing a particular kind of subjective experience is when he or she is able to inform us through the use of *language* that this is the case. Since animals have no language, the objection continues, they cannot communicate to us of features of their inner lives or provide us with assurance of having any sort of an inner life of consciousness in the way that humans can. For example, I tell the physician that I am experiencing pain in the third digit of my left foot, and this information enables the physician to diagnose the injury to that part of my body.

This objection can be countered, however, by the fact that we reliably assume that we can tell when people are experiencing certain kinds of pain, and even where in their body they are experiencing it, when their observable behavior is similar to our own when having direct experiences of pain, and that we are able to do so whether or not people inform us with language that they are having such an experience. I jump wildly around on my right foot for instance, with a pronounced grimace on my face and an evident gritting of my teeth while grasping the third digit of my left foot, and you immediately conclude that I am probably experiencing pain there. It seems abundantly clear, therefore, that not all reliable human communications of subjective experiences need be conveyed by the medium of language. Why should it be different with the behaviors of nonhumans?

5. *A burden of proof.* When it comes to our treatments of non-human forms of life, it matters greatly whether or not those forms of life are capable of having some amount of conscious experience. It matters especially when we inflict upon a living creature the sort of treatment that would have the effect upon us of producing an experience of excruciating pain. When we haul a fish up on a dock or into a boat with a hook piercing its mouth and allow it slowly to suffocate, or when we proceed to gut it while still alive, or when we thrust a crab or lobster into boiling water and watch it writhe in seeming agony and turn vividly red, does the animal experience pain? If we think not, can we be *sure* that it does not? If we want to claim that cows experience no pain or no appreciable pain when being branded with a red-hot iron, or that young bulls have no conscious

feelings of anguish when their testicles are sliced off without benefit of anesthesia, are we certain that this is indeed the case? And are we certain, no matter what behavioral indications the animals might give, of their possible inner states? The consequences of our being mistaken in these cases are grave if genuine suffering is involved, for a creature is being subjected to treatments that would horrify most of us if they were inflicted on ourselves or any other human being.

A heavy burden of proof rests, therefore, upon those who would inflict such treatments on a member of another species on the assumption that the living beings of that species are incapable of suffering trauma or pain. This is especially the case when the assumption is routinely operative but unrecognized and fails to be critically analyzed. Can the burden of proof be satisfied? In light of the case I have already sketched for the proposition that consciousness in some degree is present in many forms of life, it is doubtful that it can be satisfied. Reasonable doubt is thus an independent consideration in favor of this proposition. It is so because the consequences of the proposition's being true are stark and indefensible when we subject an animal to treatments that might well cause it to experience acute suffering and agony, a suffering and agony that we ourselves would want desperately to avoid if at all possible.

But this is a moral objection, not a scientific one, someone might argue. Indeed it is, but this observation only serves to make clear that we need to supplement our scientific investigations and understandings with relevant nonscientific ones, and especially moral ones. The latter can give important cautionary insights into what life may be like from an animal's perspective. A science that is oblivious to moral considerations is obviously partial and one-sided, for these considerations affect and pervade our daily lives as human beings. They do so not only in our treatments of one another, but with at least some significant, non-negligible, and even urgent possibility in our treatments of nonhuman animals. To deny consciousness to the latter is to run the risk of treating them in flagrantly cruel and immoral ways. Restricting the Golden Rule to ourselves alone may extract a deeply regrettable moral price. Even the possibility of such a consequence should give us serious pause. This is the clear lesson of the burden of proof consideration. If we cannot be certain that an animal is immune to first-hand conscious suffering, we should give it the benefit of merciful doubt. This statement poses the question of what we can currently claim to know about the range or extent of consciousness among the creatures of earth.

The Range of Conscious Awareness on Earth

Much of our thinking about complex subjects is guided by models, analogies, or metaphors. When we think about electricity, for example, we envision it as a *current* flowing through a wire just as water flows through a tube. Similarly, when we have thought about our relations as human beings to the natural order, we have often conceived of ourselves as masters of an entirely subservient domain; as the apex of an extensive hierarchy of beings on earth; as clever mechanics progressively learning how to understand and manipulate complicated machinery; as the owners of properties awaiting cultivation and development; or as the conservers and harvesters of natural resources. In each case, we have tended to see ourselves as the sole subjects on earth surrounded by objects pliable to our will.

The model of our relation as humans to the rest of nature I am proposing and celebrating in this book is, by contrast, that of us as integral members of a diverse community of fellow creatures, all of whom have the essential inwardness of life, and a vast number of whom have sensations, are able to experience pleasure and pain, have preferences and interests, and exhibit other attributes of subjective awareness to at least some degree. In urging this model, however, I have not yet addressed the question of the *range* of conscious awareness among the life-forms of earth. How far down into nature does consciousness reach? What species of living beings can be said to be sentient—and thus to deserve outlook and treatment as consciously active and responsive subjects?

This is a complicated and much debated subject, and I shall not make any attempt to provide a definitive resolution of it here. Besides, any original delving into it lies far beyond the range of my competence. But I do want to make a few suggestions along this line that can at least tacitly inform later parts of this book. Vertebrates, with their compact, relatively complex brains and dorsal nerve cords, can generally be credited with differing degrees of conscious awareness and feelings of pleasure and pain. Their neurological structures and chemicals are, as I have previously noted, similar in significant respects to those of human beings. Among invertebrates, the Coleoidea class of cephalopods (cuttlefish, squid, and octopus) exhibit sophisticated predatory skills, highly sensitive suction cups on prehensile arms, tool-making ability, and large complex brains—although the brains are different in many ways from those of vertebrates.[19] Some amount of conscious awareness in these creatures is likely. Crustaceans such as crabs and lobsters have relatively simple nervous systems, but they do have opioid peptides and receptors and respond to opioids (analgesics) in a way similar to vertebrates, and this fact suggests that they may be able to experience pain. In a 2005 report to the Norwegian Scientific Committee for Food Safety, biologist Lauritz S. Sømme has this to say about insects:

> In general, insects are equipped with numerous sense organs. The brain is particularly well developed in social insects, and the size of certain neural centers can be correlated with learning capacity. Learning is also known from many solitary species of insects. Insects do not react to damage of their bodies, but may show strong reflexes to constraint. With our present knowledge, it is usually concluded that insects cannot feel pain. Still, doubts have been raised. Among invertebrates, social insects represent a high level of cognition, and their welfare should be considered during handling.[20]

With regard to the relatively simple nervous system of earthworms, Sømme concludes that they and other annelids probably do not experience pain.[21] His phrase "with our present knowledge" is an important reminder that the extent of our knowledge of the nature of consciousness and its range within life-forms, especially invertebrates, is tentative at best and subject to correction by future findings. We can be relatively safe in assuming that amoebae, bacteria, protists, mites, and other micro-organisms are incapable of consciously experiencing pain, but in our encounters with more complex forms of life we need to proceed with due caution and humility.

This does not mean that we are never entitled to swat a mosquito, resort to the use of an insecticide, or rid our home of bedbugs, ants, or rodents by extermination. The issue of conflicts of goods that arise when the well-being of one animal or group of animals may need to be sacrificed if the well-being of another—including ourselves—is to be protected or maintained will be raised in the next chapter and discussed in more detail in subsequent chapters. Not all inflictions of pain or deliberate terminations of life are morally avoidable, but pointless, needless ones can be judged to be so—to the extent that we are able with some confidence to ascertain what is pointless or needless in particular situations, not always an easy matter. Transporting a single cockroach from the kitchen floor to the yard may be a more appropriate response to finding it there than simply squashing it. Encountering a teeming number of them there poses a different kind of problem. Humans, like other organisms, are entitled to protect their environments from being threatened, damaged, or overrun by members of other species. We should be careful, however, to think critically about the all too prevalent assumption that human needs, preferences, aspirations, avoidances, conveniences, and the like will in all cases trump those of other types of organism. Implications of these cautionary notes for sport fishing and hunting, factory farming, medical experiments with animals, conservation practices, and other treatments of them will be discussed later in this book.

3

Presumptive Rights and Conflicts of Rights

[E]ven if talk of "liberating" animals and extending moral "rights" to them cannot plausibly refer to changing animals' attitudes toward themselves, it can and does plausibly refer to changing our attitude toward animals from one that regards them as beings that must be treated humanely but that are, nevertheless, fundamentally resources for fulfilling human interests to an attitude that regards animals as fellow beings whose interest in an enjoyable, satisfying life must be respected and protected in the way basic human interests are respected and protected.

—S. F. Sapontzis[1]

Introduction

Refraining from restricting needless pain on nonhuman organisms that are capable of experiencing pain is a critical moral restraint. We should keep it firmly in mind in all of our approaches to and treatments of nonhuman forms of life. But philosopher S. F. Sapontzis reminds us in the epigraph to this chapter that this constraint is not where our moral perspective on or regard for animals should cease. It should not mean simply use them as you like and consider them as pliable means to your own ends whatever those ends may be, just as long as you do not in so doing subject them to unnecessary pain.

Moral perspective and regard should extend much further, as Sapontzis insists, to include consideration of the active interests of those
beings so far as these can be discerned, inferred, or assumed, and in
particular their interest as living beings in having a satisfying and
enjoyable life. The appropriate focus of a moral outlook on nonhuman
forms of life is not, therefore, just the negative one of not inflicting
upon them needless experiences of pain—undeniably important as this
consideration is—but also the positive one of acknowledging, respecting, contributing to, and acting in accordance with the preferences and
interests integral to these beings' particular ways of life.

In so doing, we greatly extend the scope of moral (and, as I shall
show, religious) concern to include an enormous number of differing
forms of life, and we include within our conception of community
not just our relations to other human beings but our relations to a
multiplicity of nonhuman others. Our placement within the larger
community of natural beings greatly augments and complicates the
narrower, conventional view that tends to restrict the scope of morality
to human relations within human societies. This move has the effect of
making human social ethics a subset of animal ethics and, by extension, of environmental ethics since the latter bears in critical ways on
the well-being of animals—including human animals—in their natural
environments. The expansion of the scope of morality has the effect,
as Sapontzis notes, of breaking down the wall we formerly assumed
to separate "us" from "them," humans from nonhumans, and to put
in its place what I earlier termed a continuum or relative difference
of degree rather than a radical difference of kind. "The diversity of
what can make life enjoyable and fulfilling," he writes, "would have
to become a more central determinant of moral concern as we incor-
porated different species into that concern."[2]

I want to build upon the spirit of these observations by Sapontzis in this chapter by proposing three "Rs" related to the expanded
view of morality he calls for. I next propose a scheme of presumptive rights for nonhuman forms of life and especially for those with
some degree of conscious awareness. Then I introduce a fourth "R" I
associate with religion and, more specifically, with Religion of Nature.
Finally, I indicate some ways in which these morally and religiously
based rights can come into conflict, most notably as they bear on
relations between human and nonhuman forms of life. Subsequent
chapters will discuss these conflicts in more detail, and I will propose

there some principles and practices that can be of use in addressing them and seeking to resolve or mitigate them, or at least bring them into some kind of more equitable balance.

Three Rs of the Thou of Nature

Envisioning and developing a thou-focused ecological ethic require, first, *recognition* of the inwardness and thouness involved in all forms of life, and especially in those where sentience or conscious awareness is present in at least some degree. Such recognition means drawing a distinction between nonliving forms of matter and those bodily systems that are alive. It means understanding that the two should not be regarded entirely alike or treated alike. Techniques of purely objective, external investigation and manipulation are appropriate for the study of nonliving matter and for many aspects of living bodies, but a full understanding and appropriate treatment of living beings demand cognizance of the inwardness of life, an inwardness that cannot be adequately comprehended in external, third-person ways. It can only be comprehended when viewed from the perspective of our own inwardness as conscious forms of life. Were we not conscious, we could not even raise the question of the manner or degree of consciousness in other living beings. Nor could we recognize signs of consciousness in these beings, however varied or exotic their distinctive modes of consciousness might be.

This comprehension requires more than intellectual acknowledgment. It requires strongly felt empathetic and emotional awareness of a shared subjectivity and mutual inwardness. Even the most elemental life-forms are much like us in the critically important fact of their inwardness, and the more complex ones share in our capacity for and experience of sentience. Proper relations with and adequate understandings of other forms of life demand on our part, therefore, an appropriate measure of *intersubjective* approach and attitude, and not an approach where our subjectivity is assumed to stand in sharp contrast with other life-forms' exclusively outward characters and modes of life and behavior, and to require for their optimal comprehension only resolutely objective techniques of analysis.

Extreme poles of objectivity and empathy can be illustrated with two examples. The first is a photograph I recently viewed of former

President of the United States Theodore Roosevelt, taken during an African safari.[3] He is posing triumphantly, holding upright in his right hand a high-powered rifle and standing behind the freshly killed carcass of a huge rhinoceros. Roosevelt was a study in contrasts, a paradoxical character in many ways. One of the most puzzling was his important and unsurpassed leadership and accomplishments in the area of natural conservation, in contrast with the evident delight he took in killing animals—especially large animals—and celebrating them as trophies. He was in this second way a disturbing paradigm of a human being who seems to lack sufficient empathy with other life-forms. In 1905, a bear hunting expedition was organized that involved Roosevelt during his presidency. Anxious to appear in the best light as a hunter, Roosevelt told a friend "that the first bear must fall to my rifle. This sounds selfish, but you know the kind of talk there will be in the newspapers about such a hunt, and if I go it must be a success, and the success must come to me."[4]

The other example is taken from Aldo Leopold's *A Sand County Almanac*. Leopold graphically describes the moment of awareness in which he suddenly recognized and understood the radical interdependencies of animal and plant lives and could no longer look at them in a purely detached, dispassionate manner. He and some fellow hunters are in the mountains looking for deer to shoot. While eating their lunch, they see an animal fording a turbulent stream below the rimrock on which they are seated. At first they think it is a doe, but when it climbs toward them and shakes its tail, they realize it is an old wolf. Soon the wolf is joined by grown pups that come out to tangle with her and with one another in a melee of playfulness. The hunters spring into action and fire into the group of wolves. Their combined fire is not very accurate, but the old wolf is down, and another one limps, wounded, into the rocks below. After describing this scene, Leopold writes,

> We reached the old wolf in time to watch a fierce green fire dying in her eyes. I realized then, and have known ever since, that there was something new to me in those eyes— something known only to her and to the mountain. . . . I thought that because fewer wolves meant more deer, that no wolves would mean hunters' paradise. But after seeing the

green fire, I sensed that neither the wolf nor the mountain agreed with such a view.[5]

His main point in describing this experience is to call attention to the complex patterns of interdependence among all the creatures of nature.

The deer need the wolves just as the wolves need the deer. To kill all the wolves might well mean devastation of the deer's habitat through its own overgrazing, and it could have disastrous effects on the ecosystem of the mountain as a whole, including animals and plants and their nonliving natural surroundings affected by such things as runoff and erosion. Extirpation of the wolf in state after state has shown the sad effects in his own time of such folly, Leopold explains.

But an equally deep and telling point is also suggested by his description. It consists in discovery of another kind of profound meaning of the "fierce green fire" of the dying wolf's eyes. That meaning is the inwardness of the wolf's now departing life, her existence as a subject among the gaping human subjects—an inwardness already implicit in the earlier playful tousling of the wolf pups with her and one another. As J. Claude Evans points out, Leopold was not only a fervent and perceptive spokesman for ecological relationships but "a passionate hunter," and he remained so despite his experience of the green fire in the dying wolf's eyes.[6] I am contending that becoming fully cognizant of the fire burning in the eyes of a fellow creature can enable us to become empathetic with and thereby to recognize the precious inner quality of life of members of countless species other than our own. And with such recognition can come an awakening of the second "R" of a thou-focused ecological ethic: *respect*.

Respect for the inner lives of other creatures can be engendered when we recognize the marked similarities of their inwardness to our own conscious awareness. We naturally value our own lives and ardently seek their preservation and continuing enhancements of their quality. We are intent upon experiencing as much joy, satisfaction, and fulfillment as possible and avoiding as much suffering, deprivation, and disappointment as we can. We are profoundly concerned about these qualities of life both for ourselves and our loved ones. We typically think it wrong to inflict needless harm or pain on another human being or willfully to deprive other humans of the possibility of leading a satisfying and fulfilling life. And we have devised appropriate sanctions and punishments to guard against such harmful practices. Our moral codes and legal systems are built upon and give expression to the root value of a profound respect for the quality of one another's inner lives and experiences as well as for the outward circumstances of these lives.

We are constantly enjoined to treat others as we ourselves would wish to be treated and reminded that there is no significant moral difference between one person and another, even when one of those persons is oneself. In other words, all are alike and are to be treated alike in the perspective of morality and law. When any sort of differential or non-equal treatment is mandated or allowed, a significant burden of proof needs to be satisfied and some sort of due process brought promptly into play. The presumption of respect for the life of another and for the felt and experienced quality of that life can readily be extended to nonhuman forms of life once we recognize the inwardness of those forms of life and cease thinking of them, as we sometimes do, as mere objects amenable to any form of treatment we might casually wish to inflict upon them. Examples of such treatments are the dragging of sick, injured, "downer" cows with chains, the brutal confinement of chickens or pigs to densely crowded spaces that leave no room for normal behavior or movement, or the subjection of animals to lifelong imprisonment and to repetitive, painful, invasive experimentation with no adequate or overriding justification.

Just as we have long thought and taught that there is no significant difference between one person and another so far as morality and law are concerned, we must, once the inwardness of all forms of life is recognized, begin carefully to consider whether we are entitled to exclude some or all of those forms of life from a similar respect— while paying due attention, of course, to their relevant differences as members of species different from our own and their consequent differences from us in specific capabilities and environmental conditions. There are no doubt important differences between our human form of inwardness and the particular forms of it in other species. We cannot know in specific detail what it is like to be an octopus, a rabbit, an eagle, a bear, a dolphin, or an elephant and to have experiences characteristic of members of their respective species. But we are entitled on behavioral as well as evolutionary and other scientific grounds such as those adduced by Thompson to conclude that there are significant overlaps or commonalities of such things as our own distinctive needs, fears, sufferings, enjoyments, and expectations, on the one hand, and theirs, on the other. I once walked unknowingly through a sticker patch with my dog. A sticker dropped in my boot and caused me to wince and stumble; at the same time, my canine companion yelped and began to limp. We were fellow sufferers.

If we are not entitled to ignore or be indifferent to such commonalities, then we need to begin to think about how a fitting respect for nonhuman lives can best be expressed and practiced in our day-to-day lives as well as registered in our moral deliberations and, when appropriate, in our legal systems. To be empathetic with and compassionate toward the inner lives of other creatures—especially those with some level of conscious awareness—is to recognize emotionally as well as intellectually the similarities of their inwardness with our own subjectivity and conscious awareness and to experience the need to respect that inwardness as something akin in important ways (although obviously not in all ways) to our own inner lives and to the basic conditions and concerns relating to the quality of our inner lives.

In fact, empathetic awareness of the inwardness of other forms of life and of our intersubjective relations to them can deeply inform and greatly expand our own sense of who we ourselves are as biological beings positioned in relation to nonhuman as well as other human beings and intimately situated together with them in various tightly woven ecological systems of the world. As Thompson observes, "the imaginative movement of putting oneself in the other's place . . . allows us to gain a new spatial perspective on the world, the perspective of the other. At the same time, we continue to have our own center of spatial orientation." Continuing in this vein, he writes, "empathy is a precondition for our experience of inhabiting a common and intersubjective spatial world. Empathy provides a viewpoint in which one's center of orientation is one among others."[7] Recognizing the inwardness of all life impels us to regard these "others" as including nonhuman others.

A logical consequence and natural complement of recognition and respect for the inward character of all forms of life is awareness of the urgent need for the third "R": acceptance of grave *responsibility* for ways in which we humans go about treating and relating to other living beings on this planet. The urgent need for this sense of responsibility becomes inescapably evident when we consider how pervasive and seriously threatening and damaging are the impacts on the face of the earth and on all of its nonhuman creatures of our ever burgeoning and habitat-strangling human population, our rampant and often poisonous and wasteful technology, and our to-date often callous indifference to life-forms other than our own—to say nothing of the potentially disastrous effects of these factors for the quality of life and even the future survival of our own species. Another way to depict the I-thou character of our relations as human beings with other sentient, intentional, purposeful creatures of nature is thus to speak simply of "we" or "all of us"—the tightly bound, integrally related community of fellow creatures.

It is not just such creatures as wolves, deer, and plants that are radically interconnected with one another and with their natural environments. We humans too are crucially dependent upon our interconnections with other beings on earth, and we have an inescapable duty to be responsible citizens of the whole community of living beings of which we are only a part. The present dire crisis now threatening the vitality and well-being of ecological systems everywhere on the earth is the consequence of the failure of humans to accept and act upon this responsibility. Recognition of and respect for the inward character that we share with forms of life other than our own can give richness of meaning and depth of emotional commitment to this sense of responsibility. Safina comments, "Compassion doesn't simply mean caring for poor people or putting band-aids on need. It seeks to remedy *sources* of suffering."[8] This observation applies also to caring for and alleviating the sufferings of nonhuman animals. The most significant source of their widespread sufferings and of the radical endangerment of many of their respective species is ruination of their natural environments. Human social structures, policies, and practices that conduce to this sad effect should be matters of profound moral concern.

Informed by the perspective of the three "Rs" and their rootage in awareness of the intersubjective character of our relations to other living beings in the natural world, the scope of our moral outlooks (and, in some important cases, legal systems) can no longer be narrowly restricted to human beings. They can and must be extended to include the whole of nature. We must cease regarding the living creatures of nature as mere manipulable, external, objective "its." They must be recognized, respected, and responsibly treated as fellow "thous." An unthinking, indifferent, and condescending attitude of I-it must be replaced with a thoughtful, empathetic, and pervasive outlook and practice of I-thou.

When this fundamental shift in outlook takes place, we are in a position to imagine a scheme of natural rights that applies to life-forms capable of sentience, intentionality, and purpose. This scheme of rights also has important implications for features of these creatures' environments since their viability and thriving depend so critically upon the integrity and dependability of their environments. *Rights*, as I shall use the term here, refers simply to attitudes and treatments from responsible, morally sensitive human agents to which living beings with varying degrees of awareness are entitled.

A Scheme of Presumptive Animal Rights

The specific set of fundamental rights I shall present and argue for is no different in principle than the most basic rights we humans would naturally wish to have applied to ourselves.[9] They reflect ways in which we would want to be regarded and treated in a just and equitable society. The recognition, respect, and responsibility they currently express on our behalf as humans are extended in this section to all sentient beings as fellow thous. Acknowledgment of the inward character of other life-forms, if taken with utmost seriousness, gives us inspiration and basis for this proposed extension. And if the extended rights themselves are taken fully into account, a radical change in our relations with living beings not of our own species can take place.[10] The comprehensive vision I am proposing under the topic of the Thou of Nature is admittedly not the only basis on which to build a strong environmental ethic, but I am proposing it as an approach that goes to the heart of the ethical issues involved and holds promise as a potent source of ecological consciousness-raising. When nature, formerly regarded as mere object or as a congeries of mere objects, comes to be seen as replete with living subjects akin in critical ways to us humans, a radical shift in perspective on the scope of moral considerability and regard can be brought about. Let us look, then, at the list of natural rights I am proposing for conscious forms of life.

The first is the *right to life*. Conscious forms of life are presumably set upon maintaining themselves in existence through their natural spans of life. Just as we normally desire the continuation of our own lives, so presumably do all conscious beings seek to persist in their being. A determined focus on self-maintenance is part of what it means to be alive. Implicit in this first right is a second one: the *right to a healthy habitat*. Willful or neglectful despoliation of the natural habitats of conscious organisms is a clear threat to the continuation of their lives and can endanger the continuation of their species. A third right is the *right to make appropriate uses of the resources of those habitats*. Conscious organisms are entitled to their occupational niches and to the nutriments, nurture, and protection provided by those niches. Without these niches and their resources the organisms cannot survive. The niches of various organisms also exhibit the radical dependence of many of these organisms on one another. No life-form is an island of serene independence and disconnection from other organisms. And the threats to one species are often threats to many, if not all, within an ecosystem. A fourth right is the *right to prosper and flourish* within the organisms' niches or habitats. It is not enough that they be permitted merely to survive. Conscious organisms naturally seek not just to live but to live well, to attain and maintain a maximally appropriate character of life in accordance with their respective natures and one that allows for the fullest possible exercise of their native capabilities. A fifth right is the *right to reproduction of one's species and, when appropriate, to the nurture and protection of one's progeny*. We humans have a strong impulse to hold our families dear and to be deeply concerned about their future livelihood and prosperity. Nonhuman conscious beings also naturally propagate themselves and in some cases devote considerable care to the nurture and protection of their young. They have a right to do both, just as do we.[11]

An important sixth natural right clearly applies to creatures capable of experiencing any amount or degree of conscious pleasure and pain. This right is the *right to be free of needless suffering*. The right to appropriate exuberance, joy, and pleasure on the part of conscious beings is perhaps implicit in the fourth right indicated above, but the right to be free of needless suffering is extremely important and deserves recognition as a separate right. *We are not really in a position to be sure how far sentience extends among living beings.* This is a point we need constantly to bear in mind as we weigh our moral obligations to members of other species. According to Jeffrey A. Lockwood, a professor of entomology at the University of Wyoming, "There is evidence that insects feel pain," and he wisely comments, "in the face of even a remote possibility that these animals suffer, surely we are obligated to mitigate their potential pain."[12] It is also important to note, as does animal ethicist Bernard Rollin that "the overwhelming majority of animal suffering at human hands is not the result of [deliberate, malicious] cruelty, but rather, the animals suffer because of normal animal use and socially acceptable motives." Confinement agriculturalists or factory farmers, for example, "may be motivated by the quest for efficiency, profit, productivity, low-cost food, and other putatively acceptable goals," he writes, "yet . . . their activities occasion animal suffering in orders of magnitude traditionally unimaginable."[13] In other words, unintended suffering is still suffering and deserves compassionate ethical recognition and consideration as such.

In a thou-focused ecological ethic, we humans are obligated to respect and honor these six natural rights in their applications to all conscious nonhuman species and their individual members just as we commonly acknowledge in our moral systems and legal codes the obligation to respect and honor these rights within our own human sphere. Or to put the point more accurately, our human sphere can no longer be regarded as something separate from and radically distinct from that of other creatures of nature. Our respective spheres co-penetrate one another and are dependent on one another in countless undeniable ways, as we can now clearly see from an ecological perspective. This co-penetration and mutual dependency, I am arguing here, involves multiple types and modes of inwardness, and not just our supposedly privileged inward awareness in relation to a purely outward nature. Recognition of the pervasive presence of inwardness in the creatures of nature justifies, in its turn, an extension of many of the natural rights we presume for ourselves to all forms of conscious life.

Philosopher Peter Singer has done admirable work in extending the scope of ethical considerability and concern to all sentient beings, arguing that it is morally wrong to inflict on them, or to allow to be inflicted upon them, needless suffering and pain. As a utilitarian, he also contends that "there are no exceptions to a rule such as: 'Do what will, in the long run, do most to satisfy the preferences of all affected by your action.'"[14] This rule includes the natural preference not to experience needless pain, and it also includes, I am arguing, the other rights listed above. For Singer, the rule applies to all sentient beings and not just to humans. He also argues that "some version of utilitarianism" follows from "the 'Golden Rule,' or the idea of putting yourself in the position of all those affected by your action."[15] I have argued in similar fashion here, even though I have not explicitly recommended any species of utilitarianism. All conscious beings are entitled to moral considerability in light of these six rights and the first three Rs I have defended, and the fourth R gives recognition to their profound religious importance and value as well.

But to return to Singer's language, can all conscious beings be said to have *preferences* that should be morally recognized and honored? I believe that they can. The preferences do not have to be experienced or entertained with crystalline conscious awareness to be present in organisms. They are present in the form of typical modes of feeling and activity of organisms as they live out their lives in their environmental settings. They *prefer* to live, as it were, in ways conducive to and supportive of their characteristic modes of functioning, striving, surviving, and thriving in those settings. It is in the nature of life itself to do so. Since this is the case, there is ample reason to include all conscious life-forms, however minimal their conscious awareness, within the scope of moral regard and moral action. An extended Golden Rule or an expanded application of Singer's "preference utilitarianism"[16] ought by all odds to include these life-forms as well. Their inwardness is akin in significant ways to our own.

A Fourth R of the Thou of Nature

I now want to highlight a fourth "R" that can provide additional context, nuance, and justification for these presumptive rights. This fourth "R" is *reverence*, and it has a distinctively religious significance. The comprehensive vision of the Thou of Nature has, therefore, a crucial religious as well as moral meaning. As I shall endeavor to show in this section and elsewhere in this book, Religion of Nature provides one compelling way in which this complementary, supportive religious meaning can be brought into sharp focus.

The idea of the Thou of Nature and its implication of a crying need for us humans to envision and practice an I-thou relation with the other living beings of nature is intended to give expression to a naturalized version of Jewish theologian Martin Buber's famous plea for an I-Thou relationship between humans and God.[17] As I noted in

Chapter 1, the version of religious naturalism I call Religion of Nature has no place for God, to say nothing of a personal God, because the focus of its religious conviction, commitment, and devotion is nature itself. There is nothing supernatural in its arena of concern; all that is religiously important and compelling is located in nature alone. And since it incorporates no conception of an indwelling or encompassing God or *Theos*, it should not be seen as a version of pan*theism* or panen*theism*.

However, the consequence of this wholly naturalistic orientation is not that human subjects are placed in relation to a nature to be regarded solely as an "it," for nature as we encounter and experience it here on earth includes not only us human subjects but a plethora of other beings whose lives give them an essential quality of inwardness and, in innumerable particular cases, varying degrees of subjective awareness. In the perspective of Religion of Nature, therefore, while we do not have an I-Thou relation and responsiveness to a personal God, we can have an I-thou relation and responsiveness to aspects of nature itself.

Years ago, when I was studying in a Protestant theological seminary, our professor of Christian ethics, Paul Lehmann, posed a question about the origin and nature of the universe. "Which is more preposterous," he asked, "to view the universe as its own explanation and basis—with all of its intricacy, complexity, variety, and wonder—or to view it as the deliberate creation of an intelligent, caring, personal God?" He obviously meant for us to respond, "Regarding it as created and sustained by God is far and away the less preposterous of the two hypotheses!" And so presumably did all of us students at that time and in that place. But as I reflect respectfully now on my teacher's question, I am inclined to think that the less preposterous hypothesis is that nature is its own explanation and ground, and that it sustains itself and all of its immense changes through time by virtue of its own immanent principles and powers. This conclusion is not the less preposterous one for me *by much*, however. The mystery of nature certainly matches, if it does not exceed, the mystery of God. There is a sense of unspeakable wonder and amazement in my present naturalistic response to Lehmann's searching question, a response that stirs in me resonances of profound reverence and awe.

I was sitting outside a restaurant with my wife awaiting a table for breakfast when I noticed a bird's feather that had somehow attached itself to one of the posts supporting the roof of the porch where we were seated. The feather was wobbling in the slight breeze of a summer morning. That feather started me meditating on the theory of evolution. Somehow, according to this theory, through millions of years of evolution birds evolved who were able to take to the air with wings, with especially strong muscles attaching these wings to the birds' sternums, with hollow bones for lightness of weight, and with delicate, downy, but quite serviceable feathers covering their bodies and wings. Once evolved, birds plied the air with elegant ease long before humans began to master the secrets of flight. This is just one of many forms of adaptation by evolving organisms to their environments, and it has all taken place through laws, forces, processes, and potentialities in nature, with no need for aid from anything beyond nature.

And here I was, as one outcome of that same evolutionary process, trying to comprehend it. I found as I meditated that morning that I could not adequately do so. It is too astounding. It is certainly a preposterous hypothesis in its own right, at least to some significant extent, with many things simply taken for granted and others not entirely explained. Yet I am inclined to believe it. To a marked extent, this hypothesis is the more amazing of the two now under consideration. It is one thing to think of a being similar to us in character, although far beyond us in capability, having created this world and all that is in it, and now presiding over it with conscious care. It is quite another to view ourselves as just one kind of creature spun off of evolution in the same manner as are all of the other countless forms of life on earth. I have to agree with Phil Oliver's observation: "The more we learn of our own evolutionary epic and the rich and growing complexity of life, the more we will have to say about the numinous nature that is our native habitat. But we can be confident and grateful that life will always exceed and overspill our words and, when they lure us into confusion of insubstantiality, will beckon our return."[18]

Theists might characterize this second thoroughly naturalistic notion as requiring untenable belief in a "more" coming from the "less" of nature, given that we are presumably so far advanced over other creatures in nature, and argue accordingly that our existence can be accounted for only if we posit an even greater, far more intelligent personal being than ourselves, namely, a conscious God with infinite capacity and infinite attributes. Out of an everlasting and infinitely wise divine consciousness and intention come the principles and laws of physical nature, material entities of all kinds, and all forms of life in nature, including the conscious lives of us humans, this counter argument confidently maintains. In other words, the supreme wonder of consciousness must be posited as primordial, not as something derivative or evolved. And the entirety of nature can most reasonably be explained as created and maintained by something more ultimate than itself, a supremely conscious personal being that has always existed and always will. Nature and especially the splendor of our own conscious awareness require a ground, and that ground is God.[19]

In contrast, the theory of biological evolution and the theories of cosmological and terrestrial evolution familiar to us from contemporary science teach us that the inexhaustible, everlasting "more" is nature and that we humans are the finite, transitory "less," that is, only one of its innumerable past, present, and potential forms of life. Our species came into existence around two hundred thousand years ago, meaning that we have been on earth for a comparatively few moments in the three and a half billion years of terrestrial time, to say nothing of the much more enormous sweep of cosmological time. Were we to cease to be, as have so many now extinct species of the past, nature would continue to be; and it would continue to do the astounding, irrepressibly surprising and creative things it does without us. It did so before, and it will do so forevermore. Is this not in many ways the more impressive, more startling, more mind-numbing, and yet finally the more persuasive scenario—the personal arising through evolution from the originally impersonal and existing as but one of the multiple, ever-evolving products of that immensely creative process and power?

The question is an open one, and I do not mean to deny the force of alternative answers to it. But the response to it of Religion of Nature is unqualifiedly affirmative. It is made with stirring feelings of reverence and with unshakeable conviction of the ultimacy of nature from which everything comes and to which everything returns. When so regarded, nature is holy. As its own ground, it is sacred ground. The response of other forms of religious naturalism would presumably be similar.[20] What implications does such a response have for the Thou of Nature, for our attitudes toward and treatments of the earth's nonhuman forms of life? How does this religious outlook of reverence for the sacredness of nature tie in with the basically moral outlook I previously sketched under the rubric of the first three Rs?

To have an attitude of religious reverence toward something is to regard it with an extraordinary kind of respect and esteem and to experience an urgent need to respond to it with wholehearted devotion, commitment, and concern. Moral values and aesthetic experiences can contribute to and give expression to religious reverence as so described, but they cannot substitute for it. Religious reverence, in its turn, can impart a depth and richness to moral values and aesthetic experiences, and provide a larger, more encompassing context within which they can find their expression. The demands of morality appeal to those things that can be accomplished by acts of the will, including the volitional development of moral character and disposition, and aesthetic experiences have to do basically with certain distinctive kinds of emotional response and awareness with their own type of cognitive character. Religious reverence can give powerful context, vision, and incentive for moral action, and it can provide significant inspiration and content for aesthetic expression.

Religious acts centered upon ultimate objects of reverence such as God, the gods, Brahman, śunyata, the Dao, or nature itself are acts of one's whole being; they are acts of intense commitment and resolute faith. They inform at the deepest level of one's existence how one conceives of oneself and the universe, how one lives, and what one aspires to become. Religious acts centered on objects of reverence include more than moral prescriptions and demands or impulses toward aesthetic appreciation and expression, important as these things are. Religious acts and responses are, among other things, ways of coming to terms with the deep challenges and stubborn realities of life beyond the control of one's will such as one's thrownness into the world in a particular time and place, with particular parents and in a particular community, society, and culture; one's inheritance of distinctive capacities and limitations, susceptibilities and weaknesses, interests and needs, that help to direct and define the course of one's life; the ever-present danger to oneself and others of incapacitating accidents or diseases; and the contingent, unpredictable finality of one's own death and the deaths of those one has come to love.

Also not lying wholly within the orbit of one's will but typical of religious outlooks and experiences are an openness to and grateful reception of unearned, unplanned, unexpected mercies and gifts, some of them significant enough to alter one's life; a sense of forgiveness and self-forgiveness for past wrongs and new hope for the future; the eventual attainment of a strangely restful, deep-lying assurance, confidence, and joy concerning oneself and one's role in the world; and the desperately needed but mysterious gift of empowerment for undertaking and seeking to realize pervasively important, life-defining goals and ideals for oneself and for others—and for being able finally to make significant headway in doing so in the face of the potentially debilitating seductions, menaces, and frustrations of evil lurking in oneself, in others, and in social institutions.

What does all of this have to do with the Thou of Nature and with the stance of Religion of Nature with regard to it? For Religion of Nature, nature itself, as we have seen, is the religious ultimate. It is that which is sacred, holy, and inviolable above all else. And the living beings of nature, most particularly those capable of sentience, partake of, participate in, and exemplify that supreme religious character and value. Recognition, respect, and responsibility are to be accorded to them, not just as moral values, but as deeply religious ones as well. They are to be regarded and treated with reverence as sacred beings of incalculable worth and significance.

Furthermore, it is in relation to the whole of nature that, in the perspective of Religion of Nature, we can expect to find our inspiration, challenge, and repose as human beings. Whatever gifts of mercy, grace, or empowerment we receive, we receive as gifts of nature. There is a power of goodness and renewal lying within us that is a gift of nature. We can give unceasing thanks, not only for the gift of our own human lives, but for the gift of being able to live in the midst of so many nonhuman forms of life, fellow creatures of nature like ourselves. As members of this vast community of natural beings, many of them possessed as we are of sentience, intentionality, and purpose, and all of them, like us, creatures of the inviolable sacredness of nature, we have both the privilege and duty of being responsible, caring members of this community. We are at home here and need not pine for some other realm. All of the members of this community of creatures deserve mutual aid and support, and none are to be dismissed as having only instrumental value. The intrinsic dignity of all forms of life, and especially of those capable of some amount of conscious responsiveness and awareness, derives ultimately from their religious value, and not merely from the value accorded to them from moral or aesthetic perspectives.

We are so used to having a plethora of nonhuman lives about us that we can become jaded and even indifferent to their presence. But suppose a time were to come in the future when most of them ceased to exist? Would we not then recognize, however belatedly, how immeasurably valuable and important their existence is? Would we then not have to acknowledge how undeniably sacred and inviolable their lives are? I remember reading some years ago Philip K. Dick's haunting novel *Do Androids Dream of Electric Sheep?*[21] A central theme of this novel is the question of whether robots can become conscious beings and, if so, what sorts of treatment should be given to them by humans. This is an intriguing question. But what struck me even more powerfully about this novel, which is positioned far into the future, is that almost all animals have now become extinct. The tiny numbers that remain are hugely expensive and can be possessed only by the wealthiest of humans. Others have to be content with animal robots, that is, mere machines made to look and act as much as possible like real animals. These machines are not of course the same, and humans everywhere long for the real animals of old. The absence of animals greatly diminishes the fascination, joy, and fulfillment of human life.

But sadly, real animals no longer pervade the earth and no longer constitute a ubiquitous, all-encompassing community of living creatures to which human beings can belong. In dramatically painting this chilling scene, Dick's novel helps to bring forcibly home to us how critically important nonhuman forms of life are to us and to the whole of the earth, and how inexpressibly sacred and irreplaceable their presence is among us. If we add to this observation the fact that the novel's portrayal is unrealistic simply because, as contemporary ecological science informs us, our lives would not be possible without the support of the complex, interdependent ecosystems in which many other kinds of life are necessary parts, then we simply reinforce in this way realization of the critical importance, inestimable value, and indescribable sacredness of all forms of life.

Conflicts of Rights

Conflicts of the rights I have listed in their applications to living beings are of course inevitable. These conflicts come especially to the fore for us humans when we try to weigh the rights and well-being of human beings as over against those of other animals. It is a mistake to think that the rights of humans must in all cases trump the rights of other life-forms, but it is not always easy either in general terms or in particular situations to discern ways in which the rights of humans can be brought into proper relation with the rights of nonhumans. This problem is particularly evident in view of the pervasive presence of human beings and the effects of their presence everywhere on earth.

To think that human rights should always and without question take precedence over the rights of nonhumans I have listed is to fall into the moral error of *speciesism*, the notion that human well-being, interest, or convenience must under all circumstances be the overriding consideration. This would mean either that members of other species have no natural rights or that, even if at least some of them can be viewed as having rights to a degree, their rights are unquestionably subordinate to those of humans. Any conflicts between the rights of humans and those of nonhumans are always to be resolved, therefore, in favor of humans. This unspoken, largely unexamined, and morally insensitive rule has guided most of our treatment of nonhuman life-forms in the past and continues to underlie and influence much of it in the present.

If we assume as I do that nonhuman lives possessing consciousness in at least in some measure have presumptive rights, it is obvious that the rights of one such group of nonhuman animals can also come into conflict with the rights of other similar nonhuman groups. These conflicts are inevitable in nature and often occur through purely natural causes, but we humans have an obligation to seek to mitigate their effects when we have contributed or continue to contribute to their coming about. This is the case when a so-called invasive species of life-forms is introduced by humans, wittingly or accidentally, into an area where animals have previously resided in a more-or-less congenial set of ecological circumstances, with a general balance and stability of such creatures in their relations with one another and with their natural environments. A notorious and often cited example is the mid-nineteenth century introduction of European rabbits into Australia in order to satisfy an English gentleman's (Thomas Austin) desire to continue hunting rabbits as he had in his home country. In the absence of the customary predators in their former region, the rabbit population soon got entirely out of hand, threatening the well-being of other Australian animal species dependent on the terrain, ground cover, food supply, and other aspects of their environments severely marred and altered by the burgeoning hordes of rabbits.

Another pertinent way of illustrating conflicts of rights among nonhuman animals is the widespread deleterious effects of the introduction of mammalian life-forms into islands in the sea where large numbers of birds habitually congregate and breed. Before the introduction of these mammals by humans, either deliberately or accidentally, the birds had no such predators or competitors and had arranged their lives and the rearing of their young ones accordingly. But now humanly introduced mammals such as foxes, cats, rats, mice, rabbits, pigs, and cattle either prey upon them, their eggs, and their chicks, or endanger their nesting sites, habitats, and customary modes of life to such an extent as to threaten their survival or even in some cases to bring about their extinction as a species.

Mitigation or elimination of the effects of such introduced animals would seem to be in order to ensure the survival of the birds, which means that the rights of the former must in some ways be overridden in order for the rights of the latter to be protected and insured. Customary ways of trying to achieve this end include trapping, poisoning, and shooting, but a more humane way of achieving it would be finding out how to shrink through appropriate baits the birth rates of the invasive animals without affecting the populations of the noninvasive ones.[22] Dealing effectively with this situation on the islands also means that the rights of ranchers, farm owners, herders, and other humans on the islands might need to be overridden or compromised in significant ways in the interest of respecting the rights of the birds and other nonhuman, noninvasive forms of life. Human livelihoods and not just human conveniences are often at stake on these islands as elsewhere, and human rights deserve recognition and respect. They should accordingly be brought into some kind of balance and accord with the rights and livelihoods of the members of other species on the islands. Just how this can be done in a just and equitable manner is a daunting problem, and it is usually unrealistic to think that the islands should or could just be restored to their original pristine state in which no humans or other invasive species were present.

The rights of animals are in conflict with those of humans in numerous other ways as well. Keeping animals as pets is perhaps an allowable infringement on some of their rights, but so long as they are well cared for, the animals might, if they could be consulted, consent in many or most cases to this practice. Rearing dogs to herd sheep might be a similar case in point, as would be using a dog as a guide animal for blind persons. We might reason similarly when the sheep are used only for the periodic shearing of their wool and are treated well. When animals are captured and confined to zoos or aquariums or similarly confined and exploited as entertainment in circuses or rodeos, their rights are being routinely overridden for the sake of human edification or enjoyment. The case is similar when they are fished or hunted solely for trophies or sport or used indiscriminately or even frivolously for scientific research—with little consideration given to their welfare, and it is similar when they are raised and doomed to be slaughtered in vast numbers in order for humans to consume their meat, make use of their hides and furs, or utilize their other bodily parts such as their feathers, oils, or tusks. Among the egregious mistreatments of domestic animals being raised for food are the consignments of chickens to overcrowded battery cages for their entire lives, soon to be killed veal calves to narrow solitary crates that permit little normal movement, or cattle to congested, waste-littered feed lots in intensive factory farming, denying to these animals satis-fying, stimulating, and appropriate modes of life prior to their being slaughtered for human consumption.

I should also mention the destructive effects upon animal lives and the usurpation of their natural rights brought about by human ground and air pollution, global climate change, taking over animal habitats, gross and indifferent interference with animal migration or roaming patterns, pollution of rivers, seas, and oceans, cutting down or burning rain forests with their many interdependent species to provide ground for raising cattle, and so on. One can travel to the far corners of the earth today and witness everywhere the heavy hand of our human presence on the planet and its destructive infringements on the rights of numerous other forms of life. In all such cases, human rights are not to be ignored or routinely infringed upon, but they should also not be the sole moral consideration. Our moral and religious concern should be expanded to include the rights of nonhuman animals, no matter how difficult or inconvenient such an expansion might turn out to be. Appropriate moral and religious action is not always easy, and sometimes it can be inordinately hard.

What sorts of changes, compromises, and adjustments in human lives might be needed, then, if the rights of nonhuman creatures are to be appropriately recognized and responsibly observed? Are there any principles or guidelines that can be drawn upon as we seek to resolve or at least mitigate conflicts of rights between the human and nonhuman, or among the nonhuman, populations of the earth? These questions will occupy us in the second part of this book. They figure fundamentally in the outlook and practice of Religion of Nature, where compassion toward all creatures expresses a fit and caring reverence for their lives and their sacred character.

4

Hunting and Fishing

I cannot but have reverence for all that is called life. I cannot avoid compassion for everything that is called life. That is the beginning and foundation of morality.

—Albert Schweitzer[1]

Introduction

The great theologian, ethicist, physician, and musician Albert Schweitzer was convinced that all the moral principles, rules, and exhortations of the ages boil down to the precept of reverence for life in all of its forms. "A man is truly ethical," he writes, "only when he obeys the compulsion to help all life which he is able to assist, and shrinks from injuring anything that lives. . . . Life as such is sacred to him." He continues, noting that a person imbued with this kind of moral awareness "is not afraid of being laughed at as sentimental. It is the fate of every truth to be a subject for laughter until it is generally recognized."[2] In labeling this fundamental precept, *reverence* for life, Schweitzer calls attention not only to its moral meaning but also to its religious import. To recognize what he elsewhere terms "the sacredness of all that lives"[3] is not just to take on a moral stance; it is also to enter into a profoundly religious orientation and commitment. It is to think and act with a reverential awe that acknowledges the incalculable value of life in all its forms and especially in those capable of conscious feelings of pleasure or pain.

In the perspective of Religion of Nature, reverence for life means being deeply grateful for our participation as human beings in the astounding diversity and togetherness of all living beings on earth. It also implies shouldering the responsibility for compassionate and equitable treatment of forms of life other than our own. Being committed to this outlook and the practices mandated by it is to run the risk of being dismissed as dupes of sentimentality, as Schweitzer points out.[4] But the commitment requires readiness to accept that risk in order to avoid the far greater moral and religious risk of failing (or refusing) to understand and act upon the precept of reverence for life that lies, as he so rightly insists, at the heart of an authentic moral and religious life. The scope of this precept includes human beings and their relations but also stretches far beyond them to embrace all of earth's creatures and to grant them a central place in its orbit of considerability and concern. With this moral and religious stance firmly in mind, along with its elaborations in the previous chapters, I want in this chapter to raise the question of how it bears upon the practices by individuals of hunting and fishing. I turn first to hunting.

Hunting

We can look at hunting from three perspectives: those of hunting for sport, hunting as a source of food, and hunting as a conservation practice. Hunting solely for sport is the practice of killing animals as a form of recreation, killing them for the challenge and thrill of running them down either in the wild or on hunting preserves and taking their lives. It is a deliberate forfeiting of their lives for human pleasure and fun. It may also involve the displaying of them as trophies, a boasting that incorporates celebrating the sizes of the animals killed, their ferocity, their rarity, their many-pointed antlers, or the like. The hunting may be done at great distance with high powered rifles equipped with scopes, or it may be accomplished closer at hand. To increase the challenge and evidence of skill, it may even be done with a bow and arrow. Less skilled hunters may succeed only in wounding animals rather than killing them outright, meaning that the animals are doomed to suffer and probably to die later on. If the sole purpose of hunting is human challenge, celebration, and enjoyment, and animals and their lives are regarded as mere means to this end, it is hard to see how it could be justified in light of the moral and religious perspectives being brought into view in this book.

But suppose this is not the principal end of hunting? Suppose hunting can have a more exalted purpose, particularly when the practice of hunting involves the eating of the animal that has been hunted? J. Claude Evans argues that "hunting . . . provides a kind of participation in the process of life, with its ebbs and flows, its intertwining of life and death that our society tends more and more to insulate us against."[5] According to him, hunting can help us humans to be more deeply aware of ourselves as natural beings participating in a world of other natural beings and can teach us to avoid the delusionary anthropocentrism of viewing ourselves as somehow outside the network of interdependent beings that runs throughout the whole of nature. For him, hunting can add to our respect for the members of other species even as we proceed to hunt and kill them, especially if we kill them for food. In so doing, we register our respect not just for individual animals but for the whole entwined system of which we and they are parts.[6]

Hunting for Evans, therefore, is not just recreational or entertaining but can have deep ethical and spiritual meaning and value, at least for some persons. He sums up his position in this way: "In hunting one can experience the integrity and wholeness of both a system and an individual animal as part of the system, even as the hunter, as part of the system, attempts to appropriate, to kill and eat, that animal. The entire experience can be an encounter with, an expression of, and a contribution to the integrity and wholeness of the natural world."[7] Perhaps so, but Evans seems to place an undue and to me baldly anthropocentric amount of emphasis on the value of hunting for us humans and to exhibit relative indifference to its obvious disvalue for the animals being hunted. Suffering and death are of course widespread in nature, but I can see no justification in *adding to them* by our actions when they can be avoided and have no clear purpose other than our own gratification or even our own edification. I find no consistency between sport hunting, on the one hand, and the fundamental moral and religious precept of reverence for life, the other three Rs, or the six presumptive natural rights of living beings presented earlier, on the other hand.

The act of eating the animal killed in the hunt is thought by some, including Evans, somehow to justify the killing, on the ground that killing and eating one's prey is rampant in nonhuman nature. For a human to act as predator is therefore for him or her to exhibit the action of a natural being and forthrightly to affirm his or her oneness with the interdependent web of nature. This argument is specious, however, because there is meat aplenty available in stores for most people in developed countries. They do not need to hunt in order to obtain it. Moreover, as I shall emphasize in the next chapter, meat is not even an essential part of a human diet. Hunting that is necessary for survival is another matter, but it is not necessary for most people most of the time. It is necessary for nonhuman animals who act in their natural role as predators, and it is necessary in some cases for poor persons or persons living in high latitudes or on the margins of civilized cultures. But it is hardly necessary for the well-to-do hunter equipped with the latest equipment designed for the killing of wild animals.

If we were to refuse to hunt, would we thereby remove ourselves from the interdependent system of natural beings and express ignorance of or indifference to our own place within that system? We would not do so, because as Colinvaux shows and as we noted in Chapter 1, we humans have developed domestication and herding of animals as an alternative to having to hunt them one by one. This does not take us out of nature. It is a different way of being in nature and making use of resources of nature. Even more fundamentally, our development of agriculture makes the gathering of plants one by one obsolete, and we humans, as omnivores, are perfectly capable of surviving and flourishing on agriculturally grown plants alone.

But do the production and domestication of animals for food and the growing of plants on commercial farms increase a delusionary sense of distance and separation from nature on the part of humans? These prominent aspects of civilized life may well have that effect, and Evans deserves credit for stressing their possible outcome, as he persistently does throughout his book. But resolution of the problem need not require a practice of hunting animals. Humans can go to the woods, mountains, plains, or seashore and refresh their sense of being integral parts of nature without having to kill other beings. They can hope in so doing to encounter wild animals or even deliberately seek them out for observation, amazement, and enjoyment. There is no persuasive reason to kill wild animals merely for our pleasure or for ritualistic expression of our involvement in the processes of nature, and every reason for wanting and allowing those animals to live and flourish in their own natural settings.

There are predators and preys in those settings, of course, but I can find no compelling reason for us humans in most modern settings to be among the predators, especially not with the overpowering technology and assistance of such things as powerful rifles, specially built blinds, enticing bird calls, clever decoys, or dogs bred and trained for the hunt. We are part of the network of creatures, to be sure, but our advanced technology and particular kind of intelligence give us a radically unfair advantage over other creatures when it comes to taking on the role of predator. We can revel in the richness and wonder of nature and experience ourselves as intimate parts of nature without the need to hunt and kill. We have the choice to do so; other animals do not. I am arguing that we have both the moral and the religious duty to refrain from hunting as a kind of recreation or sport, or as an allegedly necessary or commendable way of bringing home to ourselves our intricate relationship to the rest of nature.

I also think that a case can be made for the observation that Evans's celebration of hunting is rooted in a kind of nostalgic sentimentality and romanticism of its own, a pining for days gone by and for a role of humans in the natural order that is no longer necessary or appropriate.[8] This seems to me to be so despite his repeated strictures against sentimental and romantic outlooks on nature that for him distort our rightful place as humans in a system of nature pervaded with predation. I respect Evans's book as a thoughtful meditation on and defense of the practice of hunting. Its arguments deserve to be taken into account. But I do not find these arguments to be convincing.

Evans talks in one place about the gnawing sense of guilt, remorse, and even sin that some avid hunters experience when they shoot and kill wild animals, while still admitting their deep pleasure and excitement in doing so. This kind of ambivalent feeling, he argues, should not be thought to raise any kind of serious question about the morality of hunting itself. To view it in that way would be to succumb to a kind of sentimentality or romanticism that refuses to acknowledge the ambiguities of nature itself, where predation is normal and rampant.[9] But perhaps the feelings of guilt, remorse, regret, and reservation to which he refers should be taken seriously as insightful intuitions leading to a basic moral conclusion, namely, that killing for pleasure or killing when there is no pressing need to kill, no matter how satisfying or habitual the practice may have become in someone's life, family, or tradition, is actually morally wrong and should be given up for that reason. This is not at all to say, as philosopher Joel Feinberg points out, that animals have any "general claim against humans to the protection of their lives in the state of nature where they must hunt, kill, and eat one another. Human intervention to save animal lives in the wild, in fact, would itself be a kind of cruelty to the animals whose instincts require them to kill."[10] In other words, humans have no obligation or right to interfere with the normal predatory practices in nature in order to try to save the victims of such predation. This is certainly true, and it would be the worst kind of sentimentalism to think otherwise, but I am also arguing that humans have no right to be predators themselves when such predation is not strictly necessary for their survival, health, or well-being, and when their predations are performed only for their entertainment or even in order to satisfy the desire to awaken, deepen, and sustain a sense of their enmeshment in natural processes.

But what can be said about hunting as a way of culling excessive populations of nonhuman forms of life in nature? Is it not defensible as a means to this end? An overpopulation of elk or deer, for example, can lead to severe depletions of the food resources on which these animals depend. This outcome can mean slow and painful starvation for many of them. By allowing shooting of a carefully determined number of them, the argument proceeds, such a tragedy can be avoided. Conservation agencies should welcome, therefore, periods of the year in which sport hunting is not only allowed but encouraged. And by paying the appropriate fees for the privilege of hunting, the hunters can make effective contributions to the maintenance of parks and wild areas and to the well-being of animals and the stability of their species in those places.

We need, however, to ask ourselves this question: Would we be ethically entitled to kill a certain number of humans on a regular basis in order to ensure that other humans can have food and a better standard of living? It might be claimed that we do so through acts of war, but when justified these are defensive acts against aggression, not a calculated means of population control. And we commonly condemn ethnic cleansing, in whatever guise, as a grave moral wrong. If we do not approve of the routine "culling" of humans but are willing to approve it for nonhuman animals, where does the moral difference in the cases lie? Are we humans of such immense value compared to elk, deer, or some other nonhuman creature that we are entitled to a practice regarding them we are entirely unwilling to have applied to ourselves? If so, in what does that immense comparative value consist?

It could be argued that we humans have the knowledge and intelligence to use conservation techniques on behalf of nonhuman animals that they themselves do not possess, and that we therefore have an obligation to tend to their well-being by culling their populations when necessary. Allowing hunters to gun them down with clear limits on the number of kills is one way of doing so—an example of needful killing. It could also be argued, as Lockwood does in personal correspondence, that if I were a deer or some other animal in the wild, I would prefer a swift high-powered bullet death to one involving slow suffering and starvation. This would mean that even hunting for pleasure should be allowed, not only because it can help to keep the animal populations at an optimal level, but because it may be in the best interest of the particular animal being shot. It may seem easy to legitimate regulated sport on this basis, but this reasoning can easily disguise or betray rationalization. Routine sporting hunting can breed callousness toward the lives of the animals being hunted. The fact that hunters' prey is frequently referred to as "game" gives the game away, as it were. What purports to be ethical culling can be for the hunter just a game, and the creatures to be killed just trophies of the game. When rabbits, pheasants, deer, and the like are regarded merely as game, their character as thous is put entirely out of mind.

Deliberate killing carried out in the name of culling should be a last resort, not a first one, as it is for us humans on the rare occasions when an act of killing may be sanctioned or allowed, for example, for self-protection or protection of the innocent. And it would perhaps be better to have the culling done by trained park rangers and professional wildlife managers rather than by ordinary hunters out for a good time. There is highly significant deontological aspect of the latter action that merits consideration, and not just its actual outcome. The outcome may be the same, whether conducted by professionals or ordinary hunters, but the motivations may be quite different—in the first case more likely explicitly moral in intent and accompanied with appropriate restraint and regret, in second case not as likely to be so.

Moreover, the professionals can be trained to be skillful marksmen or markswomen—and chosen at least partly on the basis of their aptitude for such training—thus mitigating in this way the likelihood of the animals' prolonged suffering when only injured by amateurish shooting. I am aware that this is an extreme suggestion and one unlikely to be given public support in the near future, but I still think it worth considering. I am also aware that this practice would mean that revenue from hunting licenses would be lost, and that this important source of funding for conservation practices would have to be set aside and compensated for in some fashion. A less extreme solution to the moral problem might be developing baits capable of curtailing fertility rates among animals in which overpopulation is a problem, a solution suggested in the preceding chapter when discussing the rampages created by humanly introduced and rapidly reproducing invasive species. This approach would be similar to the spaying and neutering of street cats and dogs or of household pets. Highly selective population baits would eliminate the claimed need for seasonal culling by human hunters. The problem of overpopulation among such animals as elk and deer can often be attributed to the human removal from their environments of their natural predators such as mountain lions and wolves. Restoring these natural predators to their places and roles would help to relieve the population problem without calling in the aid of human hunters. It is sadly the case in some areas of the United States that the natural predators of so-called game animals are systematically depleted or wiped out by wildlife officials, not just as a program for protecting livestock on farms and ranches but also in order to ensure that the game animals are abundantly available for humans to hunt and kill.

Humans have rights as well, including the right not to have their livestock marauded by predators such as wolves. This putative right—a right to protection of property—is deserving of respect, but so are the rights of the wolf or other predator, especially when its survival in fitting numbers turns out to be crucial to the well-being of the natural environment and of other creatures in that environment. The practice of having eager hunters pay large fees for the privilege and delight of shooting wolves or other possible predators on human livestock from the air seems to me to be morally unconscionable. Compromises and adjustments of rights in relation to one another are appropriate here as elsewhere. What is not morally appropriate is complete indifference to the animal rights at issue or an unexamined belief that the rights of nonhuman animals are in all cases subordinate to those of humans or to what is easiest or most convenient for human beings. Trying to live a consistently committed moral and religious life is not always easy. Sometimes it is demandingly—and confusingly—hard.

Before leaving this section, I want to take brief account of a defense of speciesism that is sometimes mounted and to which an answer needs to be given. What if your child, husband, or wife were threatened or attacked by a wild animal? Would it not be your instinctive response to save the human, even at the cost of killing the animal? And is not this response highly appropriate and correct? I think that this would in most cases be the right response, just as in a similar extreme circumstance I would be justified in taking the life of a human aggressor. But in neither case would I do so without regret for the life that is taken or acknowledgment of the need to satisfy an appropriate burden of proof. The rights of both parties are at stake, and the right of one is being sacrificed in order to protect the right of the other. But once again, it is not at all clear to me that the rights of humans, whatever threats to them might arise in particular cases, must in all cases override those of other beings, and especially of other beings with some modicum of conscious awareness.

Let me now turn our attention to sport fishing. Is it significantly different from hunting? Can it be morally defended as a pleasurable, harmless pastime? Fish are certainly alive, but do they have to any notable extent the three traits of conscious awareness indicated by Thompson: sentience, intentionality, and purpose—traits to which I refer collectively as sentience? Are fish even capable of feelings of pleasure and pain? Perhaps fishing is something altogether different from hunting when viewed from a moral perspective. I shall take issue with this idea in the next section.

Fishing

Before addressing the topic of recreational or sport fishing, I want to say something about my personal experience with the practice of hunting as distinguished from that of fishing. My father tried to interest me in hunting when I was young. He took me on a dove-hunting expedition with some of his adult friends. It was mildly exiting, and I did not at that time have any moral scruples about it, but this and other such experiences did not motivate me to take it up as a regular

practice. My moral reflections about it came later, and my religious
approaches to it even later. Fishing, however, was for a long time a
different matter.

I was for many years an eager participant in deep sea fishing
expeditions into the Gulf of Mexico, and I enjoyed fishing in the
brackish waters of bayous near our family homes while growing up
and into my adulthood. I also went crabbing with my grandfather and
others on the Gulf beach near my childhood home and watched live
crabs twist and writhe while slowly turning beet red in boiling water
as we prepared them for food. I ate my mother's deviled crabs and
crab gumbo with relish. And I feasted with delight on the grouper,
red snapper, trigger fish, flounder, and other types of fish I caught in
the Gulf. While living in Delaware and Kentucky, I fished regularly
in lakes nearby, and I did some fishing in lakes and streams when I
moved to Colorado. On one occasion, while fishing in Kentucky with
a friend, his cast with a large bass plug on his line tangled somehow
with the line on my fishing pole and ended up with one of the large
hooks of his plug driven deeply, barb and all, into the tip of my nose.
Removing the hook was a long and painful procedure because the
physician who attended me held the view that anesthesia would not
work in that cartilaginous area.

Did that experience cause me to reflect on the morality of fishing? Sad to say, it did not, until much later in my life. I finally came
to ponder seriously what it would be like to have my lips impaled
on a barbed hook or to swallow a piece of bait, sharp hook and all.
I also began to ponder what it would be like to have my stomach
slit open and my intestines removed while I was still alive, or to be
allowed slowly to suffocate while being admired, displayed, measured,
weighed, or simply tossed aside. And I began to think seriously about
what it would be like to be boiled alive, desperately but futilely struggling, as the crabs often did, to climb over the rim of a steaming pot
in order to escape. Were such reflections mere sentimentality or were
they making me aware, after so long a time, of something of critical
moral and religious importance? If the responses of sea creatures to
such treatments were mere reflex actions with no conscious awareness,
I need not worry. But if they were reliable behavioral indications of
genuine suffering and pain, then I had a lot to repent of and to feel
deep remorse about. For I had treated fellow creatures, capable as I
am of feelings of pleasure and pain—and in all likelihood of intense

and agonizing pain at that—with a cruel and vicious disregard for their feelings. I had callously treated living thous as mere its.

As an example of an older and still very prevalent attitude toward nonhuman creatures, one with which I am in strong disagreement, let me tell a story about one of my fishing trips with my father in the Gulf of Mexico. It was a Sunday morning, and we had booked aboard a fishing boat that was to head far out into the Gulf. The boat left its mooring at 4 a.m. and did not return to it until sundown. The two of us were met at the gangplank by the boat's captain. He greeted us warmly and pressed into our hands extremely small copies of the New Testament. He directed us to the central cabin of the boat, in which chairs had been set up in rows for its fishing passengers. When all of them were seated, the captain began a lecture whose theme, as he announced it, was "dominion over the creatures." After talking for a few minutes, he told us that he was going to clap his hands. As soon as we could do so, he instructed, we were to clap our hands after him. We tried to do so, and he complained that we were not nearly quick enough. We practiced over and over until we were at least able to satisfy him with the speed of our responses. The purpose of the exercise, he explained, was that as soon as we felt a nudge of our hooks deep in the Gulf, we were to set the hook. We had to be quick, or we would lose the fish. We were entitled to have dominion over the sea creatures, but we had to learn how effectively to exercise this dominion.

Later in the voyage, when someone would pull to the surface an especially impressive specimen from the dark waters below, the captain would hold up his hands and exclaim, "Praise the Lord! Dominion over the creatures!" My father succeeded in catching a much bigger grouper than I did, and he slyly insinuated that he was more blessed by the Lord than I and that he had mastered the technique of dominion over the creatures more expertly than I had. We laughed about the experience on the fishing boat in coming days and enjoyed telling the story to family and friends. But as I reflect on it now, it fills me with feelings of sadness. Those marvelous sea creatures were going about their business one-hundred feet down in the Gulf, and we humans deceived and bullied them to the surface just for a day's fun and relaxation. We did not need to eat the fish, and when we returned to the dock we sold most of the ones we had caught. We treated them as mere means, in total obliviousness to their own ways of life and in reckless indifference to their highly probable capacity for suffering and pain. "Dominion over the creatures" I now see as a nefarious doctrine, at least as we viewed it and put it into practice that day. Sanctioned in the name of the captain's religion, his interpretation of the doctrine seems to me to be—at least from the perspective of my own Religion of Nature—fundamentally immoral and irreligious. In saying this, I do not mean to be disrespectful toward his or other people's religious outlook, and I gave at least tacit assent to a similar view for a long time. But I do want to register here as forcefully as I can my current conviction about the matter.[11]

Do fish and other sea creatures have feelings? Can they experience pleasure and pain? Is there a conscious dimension to their lives? Much debate surrounds these questions at present, a lot of it in the form of dismissals of positive answers to them by organizations and publications that promote sport fishing. I now come down squarely on the affirmative side of answers to such questions because as I indicated in Chapter 2, in view of the behavioral indications of fish when subjected to treatments I am describing, a *burden of proof* rests on those who would deny that these behaviors give any evidence of real pain. It does so especially when, in a mood of compassionate empathy, we put ourselves in the place of creatures undergoing such treatments. Scientific evidences of a total absence of pain in these creatures under these circumstances would have to be extremely compelling for me to acknowledge its absence.

Moreover, there is a widely cited scientific experiment that gives strong evidence that fish do experience pain. The experiment was led by Lynne Sneddon of Liverpool University and published by the Royal Society in 2003. Areas around the mouths of rainbow trout were injected with bee venom and acetic acid, and their subsequent behavior was observed. Fifty-eight pain receptors were detected in the vicinity of the mouths of the trout, and they were found to be more sensitive in this area than humans. After the injections, the fish rubbed their lips on the bottom of their tank and against its walls, and exhibited a rocking motion similar to that of other animals when experiencing stress. Their opercular (gill cover) beat rate was significantly increased. They also took over twice as long to resume feeding as did a control group. In the judgment of the experimenters, the study indicated that the fish under investigation were definitely capable of experiencing pain.[12]

Not all scientists agree with the conclusion drawn by the scientists in this study, but the study and others similar to it[13] add convincing force to implications of the everyday observable behaviors of fish when caught which seem to indicate that sport fishing causes real pain in the creatures on which it preys. These two kinds of evidence, when accompanied by the burden of proof argument, cast serious doubt on the morality of sport fishing. The doubt is not reduced or removed in the practice of catch and release fishing, because it inflicts trauma on fish not even intended for food but caught entirely for the challenge and thrill of capturing, exhibiting, and admiring them before they are returned at last to the water. In the meantime, they are deceived by what looks like available food, impaled on a hook, dragged protesting and resisting through the water until near exhaustion, and brought abruptly into an asphyxiating environment, there to be handled by strange members of another species. This would seem to be a clear case of inflicting needless anguish on a fellow creature for no reason other than human entertainment or gratification, yet Evans defends the practice of catch and release fishing on grounds similar to those he adduces in defense of hunting.[14] Fishing is, in the final analysis, only another kind of hunting—in water instead of on land—and the moral objections I have raised to sport hunting also apply to sport fishing.

Carl Safina is an extremely sensitive environmentalist and ecstatic lover of the wonders of nature, and his book *The View from Lazy Point* makes this fact abundantly and eloquently evident. But he also loves to fish, and at one place in his book he readily admits to pangs of conscience when he fishes at night for striped bass with a friend, using live eels caught in traps with horseshoe crabs for bait. The eel numbers are down by as much as 99 percent from what they were fifty years ago, he observes, and the newly maturing horseshoe crab numbers dropped nearly 90 percent between 2001 and 2003 in Delaware Bay. "Tonight I'm trading standards for expediency, a classic slippery slope." He says of the eels he is using for bait, "For catching big fish, they're high-quality bait. For your conscience, low quality."[15] In another place in his book, Safina comments: "For all I appreciate about fishing, there is no hiding the fact that its basic premise is unfair deception. It has another fundamental drawback: it's not much fun for the fish. The correct mental posture for fishing always keeps that fact in mind."[16]

It is clear from these honest musings of Safina that "the correct mental posture" might be refraining from sport fishing altogether, given that his fishing is not necessary for his survival and that it elicits in him such (I would say quite appropriate) moral misgivings. To give up such an enjoyable and deeply engrained practice would no doubt be extremely difficult for someone like Safina, and I do not presume to judge him. It took a long time for me to come to this conclusion and even longer to act upon it. As I have remarked repeatedly, consistent ethical practice is not always easy. Safina himself makes this point compellingly when he remarks, "All of us have compulsive loves we must forebear. We forget to see that we can engage the world without harming it."[17] My deep desire in writing this book is that serious consideration be given to the idea that the compulsive love of sport hunting and fishing that has for so long been endemic in our culture—a compulsion of which I myself have long been a victim—ought now to be replaced by a powerful new impetus of considerate love and concern for the unimpeded lives and welfare of the nonhuman animals of earth, whether they dwell on land or in the sea.

Responses to the Charge of Impractical Idealism

Am I indulging in wildly impractical idealism when I urge that we consider forbearing, on moral and religious grounds, such ancient and deep-seated practices as recreational or sport hunting and fishing? Must we give up the thrill and challenge of the hunt or the rich and ancient satisfaction of preparing and feasting on one's prey? Do I really want to urge that we reject as immoral the familiar picture of the young lad with his straw hat, his long cane pole, and his can of freshly dug earthworms sitting on the bank of a quiet pond on a warm summer's day, or the tranquil image of the rubber-booted fly fisherman skillfully casting his line for darting trout in a bubbling stream? Is not such a proposal far too outlandish and extreme? I have two comments to make in response to these questions.

The first one is that neither morality nor religion should shrink from the resolute pursuit of ideals. Ideals that once seemed impossible to attain at one time may, by unstinting effort and gradual awakening of awareness, be attained or at least much more closely approximated at a later time. Examples are the abolition by Parliament of the highly profitable slave trade and of the institution of human slavery in Great Britain, the achievement of women's suffrage in Great Britain and the United States in the face of fierce opposition and after a prolonged struggle, and the eventual establishment of laws banning open and rampant racial discrimination in the United States. Each of these moral and legal achievements was once regarded by most people as unattainable and impractical ideals in view of the formidable, long established individual attitudes and institutional practices seeming to stand inexorably in its way. Only a few visionaries dared to think differently, and they produced through protracted labor and committed leadership massive changes in human outlook and behavior. So ideals and idealists can sometimes turn out to have immense practical value. They can change the world.

Despite the stubborn, seemingly intractable difficulties with which his compassionate, comprehensive philosophy of animal liberation is confronted, Singer rejects the view that it is "a mere utopian ideal." He readily admits that "it is a demanding ethic that virtually no one will entirely live up to," but he states that it "remains the guiding source" of his moral outlook.[18] The same thing can be said of the moral and religious outlook I am proposing here and elsewhere in this book. It is hugely demanding and places ambitious and expansive ideals before us. These ideals will admittedly never be perfectly realized, partly because they run against the grain of so many entrenched assumptions, habits, and practices, and partly because they require continuous difficult and often highly debatable (and currently much debated) assessments, adjustments, and negotiations of conflicting outlooks and values. Also, mine is far from being the only available moral or religious perspective.

I do not want to minimize in any way the formidable obstacles and challenges such ideals would impose on us individually, socially, and as matters of public policy. What progress we make toward their attainment will no doubt be slow and marked by considerable controversy and stubborn resistance. Meaningful progress has already been made in this direction by enactment of appropriate legislation for animal welfare, as Paul Waldau's book *Animal Rights: What Everyone Needs to Know* makes encouragingly clear, but much more remains to be done. Ideals such as the ones I am setting out in this book can be a "guiding source," to use Singer's phrase, as we work for a more just, compassionate, and equitable world—a world that includes and requires focused moral and religious consideration for the diverse forms of life on earth and not just for ourselves or our own species.

I am not proposing for now or for any foreseeable time in the future a legal prohibition of sport hunting or fishing. Advocacy of such a policy would not only be hopelessly naïve, it would run roughshod over the sensibilities and reasonings of the manifestly large numbers of people who do not currently share my thinking on these matters. It would invite, moreover, the kind of unbridled abuses characterizing the prohibition era in its futile efforts to eliminate by law alcohol consumption in the United States. But I am arguing the need for much greater awareness and more attentive consideration of the moral and religious issues involved.

My second comment in response to the charge of impractical idealism is simply to point to the eminently practical consequences for us humans of the kind of consciousness-raising I am recommending in this book. An attitude of wholesale indifference to the well-being of the nature of which we are an integral part, and of treating other creatures in a manipulative, arrogant, I-it manner, is bound to bring about (and is already bringing about throughout the earth) extremely regrettable and disastrous consequences not only for many aspects of nature in general but for us humans as well. The current avalanching ecological crisis is a crisis for all ecological beings, and we are part of their number. There is thus ample pragmatic justification on all sides—including our side—for the truth and value I claim for the four Rs and the scheme of natural rights for conscious forms of life I propose.

As philosopher William James asserts in his essay "The Moral Philosopher and the Moral Life," every *de facto* desire, demand, claim, preference, or need of any creature "creates in so far forth an obligation," and "the guiding principle for ethical philosophy (since all demands conjointly cannot be satisfied in this poor world) [should] be simply to satisfy at all times *as many demands as we can.*" The best act in any situation must therefore be the one "which makes for the *best whole*, in the sense of awakening the least sum of dissatisfactions."[19] Placing this insightful comment in the context of our discussion here, the best moral choices, viewed from a practical standpoint, will be those that take into due consideration the presumptive rights of all conscious creatures, including the right to a safe, healthy, and supportive natural environment. The worst choices are those that put these rights at odds with one another, willfully and routinely violating the rights of one or more groups simply in order to favor those of one or more other groups.

A familiar example of the latter is subordinating the rights of all nonhuman forms of life to human ones or ignoring these nonhuman rights altogether whenever it suits the convenience, pleasures, or wishes of human beings. This practice may seem to be sustainable in the short run, but it will finally work to the detriment of all the creatures of earth, including human beings. Relentless human speciesism is at bottom a kind of extended Social Darwinism that focuses entirely on competition and ignores the inescapable need for cooperation and mutual support, not only in social systems but in ecological ones as well. A radically different outlook and thoroughgoing revision of customary practices when it comes to our treatment of the members of other species can be of significant benefit and vital importance to us humans as well. Demanding, far-reaching, mind-stretching ideals are our necessary guideposts and destinations along the way—as necessary for us as for the rest of the community of natural beings to which we essentially and not just incidentally belong.

5

Eating and Wearing

> [I]f we feel wonder looking at a complex organism, that wonder at least suggests the idea that it is good for that being to flourish as the kind of thing it is. And this idea is next door to the ethical judgment that it is wrong when the flourishing of a creature is blocked by the harmful agency of another.
>
> —Martha Nussbaum[1]

Introduction

The purpose of moral and, as I am arguing, religious treatment of nonhuman beings is not just avoidance of inflicting unnecessary pain on them—critically important as this consideration undoubtedly is— but also an active concern for each species of animal's particular kind of flourishing or good. As Aristotle pointed out long ago, each type of animal has its own distinctive *telos* or end characterizing what is best for it, namely, its own normal, unimpeded way of developing and living. It is morally and religiously incumbent upon us human beings to acknowledge and protect the myriad types of *telos*, to the extent that our actions affect or, with no sufficient warrant, threaten or impede its optimal expression.

Philosopher, classicist, and legal theorist Martha Nussbaum, in the epigraph to this chapter, rightly ties this obligation to an awakened sense of *wonder* or what I have called profound feelings of *reverence* for each creature's typical form of life. To stand in awe at the incalculable marvel and mystery of each of the distinctive and diverse kinds of creature on earth is to experience a humbling moral sensibility and to trace the taproot of a truly comprehensive moral wisdom. It is also to experience a deeply inspiring and motivating dimension of religious awareness and responsibility. This sense of reverential wonder spills over into our moral relations with one another as human beings, adding to them a breadth and depth they would sorely lack if confined only to our own species.

In the previous chapter I analyzed the moral significance of sport hunting and fishing and concluded that these practices, widespread and customary as they have been over centuries and enshrined as they are in our cultural lore and economic institutions, cannot be morally defended or at the very least are in need of fundamental moral analysis and criticism. To hunt animals for entertainment or for an allegedly edifying affirmation of our natural state as human beings is to use them as mere means for human ends. It is to violate their integrity, rights, and sacred character needlessly and to subject them to suffering and loss of life for no overriding moral reason. Hunting may in some cases be necessary for sustenance, in which case the human being takes on the role of a natural predator, but this necessity is relatively rare in most contemporary cultures and societies. Hunting for the avowed sake of culling can open the way to actually doing it simply for morally dubious human adventure and entertainment, and it raises the searching question of whether more morally defensible means to the end of culling—when and if that end is truly unavoidable—can be found.

These moral considerations are likely to be dismissed out of hand in many quarters as mere squeamishness or sentimentalism. But when this reaction is provoked it is more often than not rooted in a tacit overlooking or insistent downplaying of the thou quality of animals and an attitude toward them as mere its. Such a response typically if only implicitly reserves moral rights to humans and neglects or refuses to grant them to nonhuman forms of life. I am arguing that the topics of sport hunting and fishing are matters for serious moral concern and that, if we have not done so previously, we need to take up the task of thinking them through and weighing their import for customary practices, no matter how deeply entrenched or habituated such practices may have become. We need to do so for both moral and religious reasons, the former growing out of compassion and communal feeling for our fellow creatures, and the latter rooted in reverential recognition of the awesome sacredness of all forms of life.

When all this has been said and done, however, an even more complex and far-reaching moral and religious issue comes to the fore. This is the issue of the human practice of eating other animals as part of a regular diet, of routinely raising them for slaughter and the production of food, and of subjecting them to the often grisly technologies and operations of factory farming and large-scale commercial fishing. In this chapter I want first to discuss this issue of eating animals and the preparations of them and their products, or the capturing of them on which the eating of some of them generally rests. In a second section, I shall consider a possible response of vegetarianism, in light of my descriptions of the treatment of animals in factory farms and industrialized fishing, and in the context of what I have argued earlier in this book and shall continue to argue concerning moral and religious attitudes toward animals. Finally, I shall address the prevalent practice of making use of animal hides, furs, feathers, tusks, or other bodily features for human clothing, ornamentation, and adornment.

Using Animals for Food

Sport hunting and fishing affect miniscule numbers of animals when compared with the staggeringly immense numbers of those affected by the day-to-day commercial cultivation and exploitation of them for our dinner tables. In most cases today, the bodies or products (such as chicken eggs or milk) of land and sea dwelling animals are made available to humans through mechanized, repetitive, rapid-production techniques that repress or give little attention to many of the natural needs or normal kinds of behavior of the individual animals involved. The older traditions of individually focused animal husbandry or of selective, small-scale, and frugally conserving ways of drawing upon aquatic populations of animals for food tend now to be left far behind. The industrial revolution has led to assembly-line, factory-like productions and treatments of animals on land in the sea. These animals tend increasingly to be raised or captured and put to use as profit-making commodities or commensurable units rather than as distinct, living, conscious beings. They have become cogs in a machinery of production.

David J. Wolfson and Mariann Sullivan provide us with this picture of the numbers of farm animals in the United States around their time of writing (2004), showing how it compares with the small percentage involved in human treatments of other groups of land animals:

> Approximately 9.5 billion animals die annually in food production in the United States. This compares with some 218 million killed by hunters and trappers and in animal shelters, biomedical research, product testing, dissection, and fur farms *combined*. Approximately 23 million chickens and some 268,000 pigs are slaughtered every 24 hours in the United States. That's 266 chickens per second, 24 hours a day, 365 days a year. From a statistician's point of view, since farmed animals represent 98 percent of all animals (even including companion animals and animals in zoos or circuses) with whom humans interact in the United States, all animals are farmed animals; the number that are not is statistically insignificant.[2]

A book by Paul Waldau published in 2009 gives us a more updated set of figures. He writes that the estimated daily slaughter figure for factory farming in the United States for one day in 2009 is "122,000 cattle, 433,000 pigs, 10,000 sheep, and 3,000 veal (male) calves." He notes that the "daily figures for chickens are not published, but the *one-day* figure if published would have been in the range of 27,000,000 (based on an annual slaughter number of 10 billion chickens in the United States alone."[3] We need to remind ourselves that Waldau's figures and those of Wolfson and Sullivan are *daily* figures and that they apply *only* to the United States. They provide only a suggestion of what the worldwide figures are.[4] This is the enormous price paid by the routine slaughter of land animals in order for human beings to be able to consume them as food. And nothing has been said so far about the slaughter of fish, either for use as food or bait, or as the massive numbers of so-called bycatches in the industrial extraction of food from the sea. Furthermore, we have not yet addressed in any detail the issue of the treatment of land or sea animals prior to their slaughtering, or the treatment of layer hens and dairy cows in the production of eggs and milk. Most of this treatment these days takes place in factory farms or by means of industrial modes of commercial fishing. Let us look first at factory farming and then at commercial fishing.

Factory Farming

Factory farming began its rapid rise in Britain in the late 1940s and in North America in the 1960s. Jonathan Safran Foer tells us in his extensively researched book *Eating Animals*, published in 2009, that "[n]inety nine-percent of land animals eaten or used to produce milk and eggs in the United States are factory farmed" and that "[g]lobally, roughly 450 billion land animals are now factory farmed every year."[5] I want first to consider the moral and religious aspects of the factory farming of animals, which for us in the United States includes all but a tiny and ever decreasing segment of the current use of animals or their products for human food, and then I shall turn to the technology of contemporary commercial fishing.

What is factory farming? Foer defines it this way: "it is a system of industrialized and intensive agriculture in which animals—often housed by the tens or even hundreds of thousands—are genetically engineered, restricted in mobility, and fed unnatural diets (which almost always include various drugs, like antimicrobials)."[6] These animals are rarely if ever admitted into the open air. They are so restricted in movement by their indoor confinement and crowding and by other aspects of their treatment such as mandated artificial insemination that they are unable to behave as they naturally would, that is, to exercise, spread their wings, forage, build nests, frolic, play, wallow, mate, nurture their young, explore, lie in the sun, and the like. Their genetic diversity is radically reduced so as to make them as uniform as possible and as suitable to human taste as possible. Their systems of growth and development are altered in order to get them ready for slaughtering far in advance of their natural ages of maturation and death, they are fed chemicals or exposed to artificial light cycles to increase the rate of their growth or production of milk or eggs, they are given large amounts of antimicrobials to guard against the likely spread of disease in their close confinement, and the structure of their bodies is modified, sometimes so radically that they cannot stand or move in natural ways, in order for them to provide the most desirable meats for human consumption at the fastest turnover rates. Their beaks are cut or burned, their tails removed, their teeth extracted, or their hooves or claws modified in order to reduce their tendency to wound one another in their close quarters. The animals frequently suffer from acute frustration, boredom, anxiety, and depression.

An article by Rod Smith in the online agricultural publication *Feedstuffs Foodlink* is entitled "Beak Trimming Benefits Welfare." In keeping with the article's title, Smith argues that the beak trimming of chickens enables them to be less aggressive, improves their feathering, and helps them to eat and drink.[7] In a similar vein, although factory farming farrowing crates for pregnant sows confine the mother into a space so small she cannot even turn around, its use is defended by farm officials on the ground that it makes it less likely that the mother pig will crush her newborn infant.[8] But both of these examples treat the *symptom*, not the cause, which is the extremely close confinement of the factory-farmed animals in the first place. The emphasis throughout is on efficiency, speed, volume of production, and the pursuit of maximum profits. Animals are treated, for the most part, as manipulable means to these ends. The natural *telos* of each type of animal—whether it be pig, cow, chicken, or turkey, is routinely ignored or willfully debased for the sake of these ends.

As I noted in Chapter 3, in quoting a statement by Bernard Rollin, these practices indicate not so much deliberate, malicious acts of cruelty as what have turned out to be socially accepted norms of treatment and near-exclusive preoccupation with economic factors in a highly competitive business environment. But the effect of the practices is enormous cruelty, flagrant neglect of animal well-being, and roughshod violation of basic animal rights. We are talking here not just about infliction of pain but radical deprivation of the fulfillment and enjoyment of these animals' normal ways of life. The physical and psychological health of the animals is allowed to count for little or nothing except as it might affect their projected value as commodities. For example, runt piglets in some factory farms are picked up by their hind legs and bashed to death on the concrete floors where they are housed. To allow them to live would be inefficient. "As in any kind of factory," Foer points out, "uniformity is essential."[9] A similar example is the routine killing of male chickens born in layer hen populations; they cannot lay eggs, so they are expendable.

Foer's book, on which much of my discussion here is based, is a comprehensive description and scathing indictment of factory farming. The book is excruciating reading for anyone with even a minimal degree of sensitivity to the integrity and vulnerability of conscious animal lives. His indictment extends not only to the treatment of animals in the factory farms prior to their slaughtering but also to deeply disturbing accounts of their reprehensible and often sadistic treatments during the slaughtering process. I shall say a bit about the latter, but I strongly recommend Foer's book for a richly detailed and carefully documented discussion of it. Much of his book is based on his personal explorations, discussions, and experiences over a period of several years.

Foer describes the process leading to and including the slaughter of chickens in the following way. The birds will be handled roughly as they are grabbed five at a time in each hand of a worker and jammed into transport crates. Working at high speed, the workers will often feel the birds' bones snapping as they load them for shipping. Even if the slaughter plant is hundreds of miles away, the birds will not be given food or water, and weather conditions are allowed no consideration. Once at the plant, more bones will be broken as the birds are hastily grabbed and shackled onto a conveyor belt. Birds will scream and often defecate in terror. The conveyor belt drags them through an electrified water bath that is supposed to render them unconscious but often fails to do so. An automated throat slitter is designed to hit the relevant arteries but often misses them. Some birds are still alive and conscious when they go into the scalding tank. "According to the National Chicken Council—representatives of the industry," Foer writes, "about 180 million chickens are improperly slaughtered each year."[10]

Cattle to be slaughtered are led through a chute into what is called a "knocking box," where a steel bolt is shot between the eyes of a cow by a pneumatic gun. This procedure sometimes fails to kill the animal and succeeds only in dazing it, either through the inefficiency of the gun or the haste of the worker compelled to work at a high line speed. According to Foer, some plants deliberately reduce the effectiveness of the knocker machine to ensure that the cow's heart keeps pumping in order to allow for a quick bleed-out time and a better quality of the cow's meat. As a result of these practices, some cattle remain conscious or awaken from the shock of knocking during the further stages of the slaughter process. They move down the line to where a worker attaches a chain to each animal's hind leg and hoists it into the air. Then another worker cuts the animal's carotid arteries and a jugular vein in its neck. The animal is then bled for several minutes. But it can remain alive even as its head is skinned and parts of its legs are clipped away in the workers' haste to keep the line moving.

The cattle that are still conscious at these stages "go wild," Foer writes when quoting a line worker, "just kicking in every direction." These practices are all in a day's work and mandated by efficiency of production. Workers who complain about them are usually fired.[11] Foer frequently refers to the lax attitudes or ineffective procedures of government inspectors relating to the practices, due in part to the speed with which they must carry out their inspections but also to the fact that Common Farming Exemptions enacted by various states in the United States allow for virtually any method of raising farmed animals so long as it is commonly practiced within the industry.[12] This ruling reminds us of the "band wagon" fallacy in logic, which asserts that if a great number of people believe in something, that makes it true. It also wittingly assigns the fox to monitor the hen house.

Foer also describes acts of deliberate cruelty and sadism performed by some factory farm workers, including those in a pig factory in North Carolina—videotaped by undercover investigators—who did such things as beating pregnant sows with a wrench, sticking electric prods in pig's ears, mouths, anuses, and vaginas, strangling them, throwing them into manure pits to drown, extinguishing cigarettes on their bodies, and the like. In another place, he cites animal welfare scientist Temple Grandin's insightful observation that workers can sometimes become sadistic from the dehumanizing effects of constant slaughter.[13] The pressures and stresses of rapid production can increase feelings of impatience, frustration, and anger toward the animals being treated in the factory forms. Unlike more conventional and now increasingly outmoded ways of farming, there is no occasion in farming factories for workers to relate to animals as individuals or in their normal settings. Respect for the animals' lives or for the subjective quality of their lives is hard to come by. In the culture of factory farming as it exists today, animals tend to be regarded as so many packages of meat or as disposable machines for the efficient production of food products such as milk, cheese, and eggs.

Writing in the *New York Times*, columnist Nicholas Kristof reports on the results of an undercover investigation by the Humane

Society of the United States of a major factory farm that produces 4.5 million eggs each day for supermarkets. The stench of ammonia rising from manure pits below older barns was overwhelming and made it exceedingly hard to breathe. Mice sometimes ran down conveyor belts, barns were thick with flies and manure in three barns, and the undercover agent reported that these barns tested positive for salmonella. Kristof notes in passing that salmonella turned up in three percent of egg factory farms tested by the United States Food and Drug Administration in 2011. In some cases, in the factory farm he reports on, eleven hens were jammed into a cage about two feet by two feet. Hens were sometimes decapitated by an automatic feeding cart as they were eating, and their bodies sometimes remained for weeks in the cages, rotting into the wiring. A spokesperson for the factory farm argued that the Humane Society's allegations were "a gross distortion," that the company is "leading the industry in replacing old barns with state-of-the art ones," and that "the reality of food processing can be off-putting to those not familiar with animal agriculture." Perhaps so, but Kristof reviewed footage and photos taken by the undercover investigator, who worked for the factory farm between January and March, 2012, and also interviewed the investigator, who "portrayed an operation that has little concern for the cleanliness or the welfare of the hens."[14]

Responding to vociferous complaints from animal welfare activists and others, some changes in treatments of animals in factor farms are beginning to take place. One example is Proposition 2, passed in 2008 in California, which among other things is designed to do away with battery cages for laying hens. According to this legislation, the hens must have sufficient room to stand up, lie down, or spread their wings without touching another chicken. Similar legislation has been passed in parts of Europe and Australia, and Kristof reports in the article cited above that the United Egg Producers in 2011 joined with the Humane Society of the United States in an agreement to support new federal standards that would provide more space for hens. Another example of progress toward more humane treatment of farm animals is the three subsequent sets of so-called Gold Standards endorsed by the Dairy Calf and Heifer Association. These standards address a wide array of areas of treatment and, if adequately enforced and put into practice, can contribute importantly to the welfare of calves and heifers. It is important for critics of factory farming to acknowledge such worthy changes and establishment of standards, even as they continue to demand much more far-reaching general changes in the treatments of animals in factory farming.[15] More honest and open dialogue between factory farmers and their critics would also be a significant step in the right direction.[16]

Industrial Techniques in Commercial Fishing

Commercial fishing has undergone radical transformations in the past fifty years or so. Sophisticated technology and high-yield methods of finding and catching fish have replaced the simpler ways of earlier times. Modern commercial fishing can rightly be regarded as factory farming at sea. Huge boats with all kinds of technical equipment can lay out longlines stretching for as much as sixty or seventy miles in length, with "snoods" or supplementary lines extending out from them, and loaded with thousands of mechanically baited hooks. They can leave these lines to bob in the sea with GPS equipment to mark their locations when the boats return. Or they can position and drag large purse seines around schools of fish that may be located by satellite generated images of ocean temperatures. Or they can employ gigantic trawling nets that scoop fish from the bottom of the sea. Radar, echo location devices, GPS location systems, mechanical baiting machines, FADs (Fish Attracting Devices), and other sorts of advanced technology make fishing on a massive scale possible.

The fish that are caught in the thousands by these means have their gills slit, once they are on the boat while they are still conscious, or they are thrown intact onto beds of ice. In either case they suffer the agony of being cut open or the even more prolonged agony of slowly suffocating and expiring on the beds of ice. They are treated in haste and en masse like slabs of meat, with no consideration given to their nature as conscious beings. Prior to their being brought onto the boat, they have been left to struggle, writhe, and bleed on the hooks; to bump along the sea bed and become tangled and injured in the trawling nets; or to be jostled and tumbled together in the purse seine nets. Many suffer and die in this manner before being brought aboard the fishing vessels. "[N]o fish gets a good death," says Foer. "Not a single one. You never have to wonder if the fish on your plate had to suffer. It did."[17]

Tim Warner, who directs the marine conservation engineering program at the New England Aquarium, observes that the seafood on the dinner plate "is not the only animal that gave its life to feed you."[18] His reference is to the extraordinarily large numbers of sea creatures brought into the boats as bycatch resulting from these modern techniques of fishing. Most of these creatures, if they have not already suffered and died, are tossed overboard. And the greater majority of them do not live through the ordeal. These bycatch animals include other fish; sharks; dolphins; minke, humpback, right, and grey whales; sea turtles; squid; rays; corals; sea birds; and members of other species, as well as severely endangered species such as some sea turtles, whales, corals, and albatrosses. Mitigation efforts have been successful in altering some of the fishing equipment and allaying some of the bycatch problem, but much of the diversity and indeed whole ecosystems of sea life are still being direly threatened. The extensive overfishing made possible and more prevalent by the techniques of factory fishing is also a serious threat to increasing numbers of marine species and ecosystems.

Our principal concern here is for the vast amounts of animal suffering and pain—both for the target catch and the collateral bycatch—inflicted by factory methods of fishing today. We tend as a people to be even less concerned with the suffering and death of fish and other forms of sea life than with that of land animals in factory farms, but innumerable aquatic creatures are doomed to suffer and die every moment of every day as a consequence of the current industrial methods of commercial fishing. All these creatures cry out for our focused attention and compassionate concern.

Why have so many of us humans been willing to tolerate animal suffering on the immense scale allowed by factory farming and fishing? There are at least six answers to this question. First, we have acquired a strong taste for meat, and especially for meat from animals technically bred, fed, medicated, and treated to make their meat as tasty as possible. Second, increasing numbers of people throughout the world want to obtain this meat at the lowest possible cost, meaning that extremely efficient methods of mass production are favored and called for. Small farms or small fishing operations are incapable of producing the desired quality of meat at relatively low costs, and they have therefore increasingly lost ground to highly competitive

factory farms and industrialized fishing techniques. It is our burgeoning worldwide demand for mass produced cheap and tasty meat that
keeps factory farming and industrial fishing in business.

Third, we have become accustomed to thinking that no serving
of food is complete without some kind of meat. This is so much the
case that it is often difficult in restaurants or the frozen sections of
food stores to find a menu item that does not contain meat. Fourth, we
tend to turn a blind eye to the disturbing facts about factory farming,
largely because the meat we eat is typically bought at grocery stores
or supermarkets where it is invitingly wrapped in clear plastic and
made barely recognizable as the flesh or product of a living animal.
Something similar can be said of the milk, cheese, and eggs widely
purchased today. They too are overwhelmingly produced on factory
farms, and we buy them, consume them, and give them to our children
without giving much thought to any unpleasant implications of this
fact. These routine practices raise fundamental moral and religious
questions, but we tend to give little consideration to these questions.
In the main, our dominant culture, governmental regulating agencies,
and the factory farms and industrial fishing companies in particular
do not encourage us to become aware of the questions or to take
them thoughtfully into account. For the most part, just the opposite
is the case.

A fifth reason is that factory farming and fishing can be highly
profitable enterprises for the companies involved in them, and these
companies can provide large numbers of much needed jobs for workers
whom they employ and who have come to rely on them for salaries
and benefits. The focus of the companies tends to be not so much on
the welfare of the animals concerned as on staying in business, and
that of the workers on keeping their jobs by doing as efficient work as
they can, and satisfying their employers as fully as they can. "Business
is business," as my businessman uncle used frequently to say, and for
the workers the ruling motto is "a job is a job." Other considerations
tend to fall far behind these two for the business executives and
workers involved, and this is particularly so when competition from
other businesses is stiff and profit margins are small, or when workers are in danger of losing their jobs if they are inclined to register
complaints about treatments of the animals concerned. Hence, most
of the emphasis is on human welfare, not on that of the animals. This

attitude is not justifiable but it is understandable, and we need to keep it in mind even as we consider the crying need for radical changes in treatments of the animals concerned. A large segment of our present economy is invested in factory farming and factory fishing.

Sixth and finally, and partly as a consequence of these other five points, we tend not to direct our attention to the fact that animals are conscious beings who are not only capable of suffering and pain but who also have active subjective lives which allow them, in normal circumstances and natural settings, to have experiences of curiosity, challenge, purpose, satisfaction, fulfillment—and even exuberance, playfulness, and joy. For us to inflict pain on them at will or wantonly and systematically to ignore and override their natural desires and ways of life solely for our culinary gratification is to raise issues of profound moral and religious import of which we are often content to remain ignorant and which we all too easily set aside.

If we give fit recognition to the moral perspective being argued for in this book, or if we enter into the point of view of Religion of Nature and that of many other religious outlooks and traditions, such ignorance is not bliss. As in the Christian Parable of the Good Samaritan, to continue in this ignorance and avoidance is to avert our eyes and pass on the other side, not paying attention to the massive unconscionable, unnecessary sufferings and slaughterings of animals that make our routine consumption of meats and other animal products possible. I would presume and hope that those theists who are confident that God has given humans animals to eat and to have dominion over would not want to claim that we are entitled to treat the animals in any way we choose, even if it inflicts massive sufferings and deprivations on them.

We should not underestimate the difficulties standing in the way of meaningful approaches to the moral and religious concerns involving factory farming and fishing, a point similar to the one made in the previous chapter in connection with sport hunting and fishing. Millions of peoples' lives and financial security rely on factory farming and fishing, as I noted above, and agencies charged with enforcing animal welfare issues in the enterprises are often not given clear mandates, budgets, or powers to be fully effective in doing so. Some agencies, such as the United States Department of Agriculture, have to wrestle with potential conflicts of interest, given that they are charged with helping to improve and maintain the prosperity of farming businesses even while monitoring the legality and morality of their treatment of animals.

There is also the weighty problem of attending to the many pressing moral and legal matters directly affecting *human* welfare throughout society, a problem that can distract from considerations of nonhuman animal welfare. And there are those who do not see any particular animal welfare problems in the first place, given their instinctive, wholesale subordination of animal to human interests or in view of their inability to recognize or unwillingness to accord to animals any significant degree of conscious awareness. Furthermore, mitigation of animal *pain*, worthy goal that it is, is also often allowed to swamp consideration of *other* important aspects of animal well-being. Hence, conceptual, attitudinal, political, economic, and priority issues tend to cloud or demote issues relating to the moral treatment of animals.

The moral and religious concerns of this book are not exactly a crying in the wilderness, but they do represent a minority voice at present. There is no easy answer to these concerns, and I do not in any way want to sound cavalier in my discussions of them. But I do think it extremely important to begin thinking about them and seeking to find ways to effectively mitigate, if not eliminate, the animal sufferings and inhibitions of natural animal behaviors involved. Uphill journeys begin at the bottom and may take a long time to make effective progress toward the top. But that is no reason to refuse starting out on them if we deem the ultimate goal to be desirable and worthwhile. And even if we can hope only to approximate certain ideals, we should strive for the closest approximations to them that we can attain. Part of this striving is open dialogue on the pros and cons of the issues involved. This book is an attempt to contribute one perspective to that dialogue.

Some caveats are in order when it comes to legislation regarding the well-being of animals and in recognition of their rights. On the one hand, we cannot wait for everyone to be good or even well-disposed toward animals before we seek to enact good laws. But on the other, as the lesson of prohibition legislation in the United States in the early part of the twentieth century teaches us, laws in a democracy cannot be effectively enforced if they lack broad public support. It is also one thing to have laws on the books; it is often quite another to find ways to enforce them in ways that actually accomplish their intent. However, we should not overlook the extent to which good laws can help to educate a populace and improve its behavior. Finally, it is of course relatively easy to write abstractly about such problems as those raised in this book but also extremely hard to find concrete ways of solving them in the real world.

That being said, however, ideas do have consequences and they do exert influences. They have an important role to play in our attempts to better the world in which we live. Formulating, envisioning, sharing, and communicating ideas (and ideals) can be a significant step on the way to their realization or at least their closer approximation. To be devoted and fully committed to nature as one's focus of ultimate concern—as in Religion of Nature—is to honor its diverse forms of life and to hold in reverence their distinctive characters and their particular sorts of developing, interrelating, behaving, and flourishing. To subordinate them, and especially those capable of sentience, customarily and uncaringly to one's own narrow interests or solely to the interests of one's own species is to be guilty of sacrilege and to succumb to a fundamental type of religious as well as moral evil. A similar observation is appropriate in the context of many other religious outlooks as well, most notably as these continue today to grow in ecological sensitivity and awareness.[19]

One way in which the plight of animals being bred, captured, and manufactured for food can be addressed by concerned individuals is vegetarianism. It can be adopted as a symbolic protest against cruel and uncaring treatments of animals in factory farming and fishing in particular or, more generally, as a way of calling into question the venerable practice of eating animals and the long established, unanalyzed assumption that we are morally and religiously entitled to eat them—given the fact that many if not most of us today can get along quite well without having to do so. If vegetarianism came to be practiced on a wide enough scale, the example of vegetarians and the resulting increased marketability and appeal of nonmeat products could have the effect of beginning to change our traditional attitudes toward animals and perhaps also of highlighting and reducing current ill treatments of them and the unconstrained breeding, capturing, confining, and manipulating of them as mere commodities or things. Let me turn, then, to the topic of vegetarianism and to investigating the kinds of defense that can be mounted in its favor.

The Vegetarian Response

We can search diligently for ways to uphold the four Rs discussed in
Chapter 3 and to avoid as far as possible infringement of the natural
rights I listed there. To cite but one salient example of a possible
way of doing so, we do not have to eat meat despite the fact that as
a biological species we are omnivores. We can get along well by eating plants, just as quite healthy quarter-ton gorillas do in Africa. The
four Rs and the presumptive natural rights of nonhuman life-forms
I have listed have decided bearing, therefore, on our dietary practices
as humans. Carnivorous animals have no choice in the matter, but as
free and intelligent agents, we do. Eating plants instead of animals
has at least five moral, religious, and practical merits that are worthy
of careful consideration.

First, the fewer animals required for our eating, the fewer that
need to be bred or captured for that purpose. The fewer animals
that need to be bred or captured for human consumption, the fewer
that must be routinely, often prematurely, and sometimes inhumanely
slaughtered, and the fewer that will be subjected to harsh, indifferent,
and commodifying treatment in factory farms or commercial fishing.
Being a vegetarian can be a personal refusal to be complicit in these
practices, and it can make one's daily diet a sustained living symbol of
protest against them. Such a symbol can sometimes invite constructive
dialogue with friends and acquaintances who are consumers of meat,
especially at mealtimes, on one's reasons for becoming a vegetarian.
Such discussions can occasion reflections on the treatments of animals
in factory farms and commercial fishing.

I have been a vegetarian for little more than a decade and did
not choose to become one until relatively late in my life. During my
time as a teacher of philosophy at a state university, we had an annual
departmental picnic to which all philosophy faculty and students were
invited. I remember asking one of our graduate students if she was
going to attend the picnic, but she replied, "And eat dead animals?
Certainly not!" I tried to persuade her that there would be vegetarian lasagna as well, but she refused to consider coming to the picnic.
She was a vegetarian, as was another student who invited me for a
vegetarian meal at another time, a meal I found to be well-prepared
and nourishing. My response to these two students was initially one of

comparative indifference or mild curiosity, even though I was teaching in a graduate program which focused on environmental and animal ethics. But over time, I began thinking more seriously about their stance and its implications.

My wife Pam, who grew up on a meat raising and processing farm owned by her father and witnessed on a daily basis the treatment of animals there, had been a vegetarian for some time when she persuaded me to become one also. My main point in reciting these details of my own experience is that the vegetarianism of these two students and my wife gradually got me to focus on and to think seriously about the moral and religious issues involved, just through the steady influence of the examples they set. As a consequence I myself became a vegetarian and am now writing about its merits as a moral and religious outlook.

Another point is also implicit in these reminiscences, and this is the fact that coming to see or seriously to consider the moral and religious logic of vegetarianism can take a long time—much longer for some than for others—and actually undertaking to practice vegetarianism consistently can take even longer. It is a big and difficult step for people who have spent their lives consuming meat at almost every sitting. Vegetarians should therefore be patient with those who may have difficulty focusing on or understanding their point of view, to say nothing of deciding to adopt their dietary practice. In presenting here a case for vegetarianism, I do not purport to occupy some kind of moral high ground but only to explain how things seem to me after some years of reflection.

Second, the raising and eating of plants is on balance more efficient than the raising and eating of animals. It enables us humans to find sustenance lower on the food chain rather than higher on it, as would be the case if we continued to eat the animals that eat the plants. If we ate corn or grains directly, for example, instead of eating cattle that are fed corn, grains, or other highly processed foods, we would make more efficient use of the calories in the food. More corn and other crops would then also be available, and often at lower cost, for directly feeding the hungry people of the world. In addition, the raising of animals for food requires much more water than does the raising of crops, and in some areas the supply of water is becoming seriously depleted.

Widespread vegetarianism could be a significant contribution, therefore, to more efficient use of resources and to easing the hunger crisis in parts of the world. Jonathan A. Foley, McKnight Presidential Chair of Global Sustainability at the University of Minnesota, contends, "We can dramatically increase global food availability and environmental sustainability by using more of our crops to feed people directly and less to fatten livestock." He goes on to make the striking observation that, "[g]lobally, humans could net up to three quadrillion additional calories every year—a 50 percent increase from our current supply—by switching to all-plant diets."[20] Energies of transporting, growing, and cooking plants (especially those made available out of season through long transport or greenhouse production) also need to be factored in, of course, but still, on balance, the greater efficiency of plant eating remains as a general rule. A possible exception to the rule is that when highly processed foods such as veggie burgers or veggie bacon are offered for consumption, the processing requires a similar amount of energy to that required to produce a pork chop.[21] But at least in the case of the vegetable products, no animal is slaughtered or made to suffer.

Evans rightly reminds us that growing crops for our consumption exacts its own environmental toll. "Every time a field is cleared to grow organic vegetables," he remarks, "habitat for wild animals is destroyed."[22] When artificial fertilizers are manufactured and farm machinery is employed, energy is consumed, and the use of pesticides means wiping out the lives of many insects and endangering the lives of other life-forms that might need them as prey. Still, eating plants instead of animals would seem to be the lesser of the two evils. As one biological species among others, we are bound to leave our imprint on the earth. But the imprint needs to be as lightly and delicately applied as possible and not allowed to become an ever encroaching, all enveloping smudge that threatens to blot out everything else.

A third argument in favor of vegetarianism relates to the amount of ground, air, and water pollution produced by the raising of animals for human consumption. Formidable amounts of methane, hydrogen sulfide, ammonia, carbon dioxide, nitrous oxide, phosphorus, and other pollutants are pumped into the air by factory animal belches, flatulence, and urine and manure deposits. The latter are often stored in large lagoons or sprayed on fields as fertilizer, where they can enter into the ground water and affect the atmosphere. The walls of these huge lagoons are also sometimes breached by such things as storms, and their contents can empty into rivers and bays, and eventually into the ocean. We are talking here essentially of open sewers and untreated materials in those sewers.

The 2011 Pew Environment Group report "Big Chicken: Pollution and Industrial Poultry Production in America" discusses at considerable length the effects of poultry raising farms on water quality in the United States, principally in the immense and increasingly concentrated factory farms in the Delmarva Peninsula. The vast amounts of manure mixed with urine produced in these facilities are spread on crop lands for fertilizer throughout this area, and they create serious pollution problems as they enter into the soil, are washed into water courses, and emit pollutants into the atmosphere.[23] Growth hormones, antibiotics, vitamins, and other ingredients in the food provided for animals in factory farming are also included in their wastes and can add their often deleterious effects to the environment and to land, air, and sea creatures—including us humans—in the environment.

Foer points out that, according to authoritative studies by the Pew Commission and the United Nations, "farmed animals contribute *more* to climate change than transport." He writes that "[a]nimal agriculture is responsible for 37 percent of anthropogenic [human caused] methane, which offers twenty-three times the global warming potential (GWP) of CO_2, as well as 65 percent of anthropogenic nitrous oxide, which provides a staggering 296 times the GWP of CO_2."[24] Bad effects of animal farming, especially in the burgeoning and increasingly concentrated practices of factory farming of animals, are not confined to effects upon the farmed animals themselves. They reach far beyond the farms to have seriously damaging effects on numerous other creatures of earth and on the health and integrity of the earth itself. A vegetarian diet can serve as recognition of this fact, count as a protest against it, and contribute, even if only a small way, to its alleviation. A significant spread of vegetarianism among humans could make a more substantial contribution to these ends.

In the fourth place, vegetarianism provides a more healthy diet than does eating meat, especially red meat and processed red meat (e.g., bacon, salami, sausages, hot dogs, processed deli meats). Heart disease, colon cancer, diabetes, and other diseases can be linked to large and customary consumptions of these meats. Reducing one's intake of them can decrease the risk of diseases that can be related to them, but eliminating them altogether can have an even more beneficial health effect. This is so assuming that the B12 vitamin and protein in red meats are supplied in supplements and in regular selections and servings of vegetable and other nonmeat sources of food. A vegetarian diet can contribute to a healthy and sustained life, while a diet high in the consumption of meats can put one's life in greater danger of diseases and premature death. There continues to be debate about how threatening red meats are to health, but less controversy about the notoriously bad effects of processed red meats. Vegetarianism avoids the risks connected with meat consumption altogether, which is why I cite this the fourth reason in its favor.

The fifth argument for vegetarianism fits closely into the overall theme of this book. The argument is that the practice of vegetarianism can go a long way toward deeply sensitizing its practitioners to the plight of animals raised, captured, and slaughtered for their meat or as accompaniments to the attaining of meat for human food. These animals are regularly and on increasingly vast scales sacrificing their lives, living severely shortened lives with radically diminished quality of living, and giving of themselves and their products with little recompense, in order that human beings can use them and their products for food. Giving up the eating of meat can express solidarity with these animals in their suffering and pain; their anxiety, frustration, and boredom; their deprivation of the joy and fulfillment of a normal life; their forfeiting of normal and normally extended lives; and their hurried, mechanical, often extremely cruel assembly-line slaughtering.

The fact that people eat several times each day means that each setting of a meal for the vegetarian can be an apt occasion for meditating on the widespread indifference to the plight of animals or on the outright resistance to seriously contemplating and seeking to ameliorate that plight—especially as it exists in factory farming and fishing—and for affirming one's resolve to continue to respond to that plight by refusing to use them for food. This daily practice can also be a constant reminder to do all that we can to protest and work against the pervasive mistreatment of animals in today's world. Eating can thus be a deeply meaningful daily ritual with vital moral and religious import for the committed vegetarian. "You are what you eat" need not be just a cliché. It has the potential to express a profound truth.

Using Animals for Apparel and Other Purposes

Humans have been using the skins and other attributes of animals in a variety of ways since early times. Their skins and wool have served as apparel and for protection against wind and cold. They have served as shelters or aspects of shelters. They have provided ornamentation, adornment, and symbolization of wealth, status, and societal roles. All of these functions are carried forward into our present societies in such things as fur coats and wraps, and leather jackets, pocketbooks, wallets, belts, chairs, sofas, and car seats. Animals are captured, raised, slaughtered, and skinned in great numbers in other to provide such items. It might be thought that the leather obtained from animals destined to be used for food is simply a by-product of food production, but actually a significant part of the profit of food producers from animals is derived from the sale of their hides. The often deplorable practices involved in producing food from animals that I have already described in this chapter are also involved, therefore, in the uses made of their hides. The tanning of leather can also have seriously damaging effects on the environment, sending many noxious chemicals such as chromium and sulfides, as well as fat and other solid wastes, pathogens, and pesticides into waterways and into the atmosphere.

Trapping animals for their fur or clubbing young seals for the same purpose also involves cruel and insensitive treatments of animals for human use. Every year hundreds of thousands of seals are killed, March to May, in Canada. The killers use rifles, shot guns, clubs, or hooked clubs as means for slaughtering these animals. The seals are sometimes not cleanly killed and may be skinned or hooked and dragged across the ice while still alive. Since six-thousand persons are allowed to participate in the annual Canadian hunting and killing, it is difficult for government agencies to monitor all of the killing to ensure that it is done as humanely as possible. The animal traps used for smaller fur-bearing animals often doom the animals to suffer for long periods of time before they die or are picked up.

In addition, animals are killed for their horns, tusks, or feathers so that artifacts made from them can be used for jewelry, accessories for hats, or other kinds of adornment. The irony is that none of this is really necessary for most of us today. We need not wear furs to stay warm; plenty of synthetic fabrics will do as well or better. We can get along perfectly well without causing animals to suffer or die in order that we can adorn our bodies. And there are entirely acceptable substitutes for leather and leather goods available. The latter function and look just as well as leather goods do.[25]

I have a wallet, belt, and several pairs of shoes that are non-leather but indistinguishable in appearance and comfort from my previous leather ones. My wife was shopping for shoes one day, and she asked a clerk if any "vegan" shoes (as non-leather ones are often called) were available in the store. The clerk replied in some astonishment (or perhaps it was only mockery), "You don't mean to *eat* them, do you?" My wife has replaced her pocketbooks, wallets, belts, and shoes with non-leather ones, and she and I are planning to shop for non-leather baseball gloves and balls to be used in our frequent throwing and catching sessions.

As for such things as chairs, sofas, and car seats, there are many non-leather materials that can be used for these purposes, some of which look, feel, and endure like leather. Even if the non-leather materials were inferior in some ways to the leather ones (for example, my wife was told by a shoe clerk that leather shoes "breathe" better than non-leather ones), it would make good moral and religious sense to use them and stop using the leather ones on the ground of refraining from inflicting unnecessary suffering on conscious animals. The same reasoning applies to shoes, boots, belts, and other items made from alligator, snake, or other more exotic skins. While we may not always be able to avoid using animal hides or other aspects of animals in our modes of dress or other aspects of our lives, it would seem to be both morally and religiously advisable for us to seek to do so as far as we can.

Such boycotting of animal products in our stores and catalogues can have a beneficial effect in reducing the amount of unnecessary suffering and dying animals undergo on our behalf. Such a practice is consistent with the four Rs and the six presumptive natural rights of nonhuman forms of life. Like vegetarianism, it can serve as a meaningful symbol, ritual, and act of protest for its practitioners; as occasions for conversations with friends and acquaintances on the topic of animal welfare and animal rights; and as an economic incentive for society and businesses to be more sensitive to the plight of animals and to produce suitable substitutes for animal products in larger numbers.

We can show compassion for animals, help to reduce their suffering, and contribute to their overall well-being in many different ways, including giving up or refusing to support sport hunting and fishing. But something closer to home and to the daily lives of all of us that we can give serious consideration to doing as an expression of moral (and perhaps religious) concern for the well-being of animals is cultivating new habits of eating and wearing. These new habits can mean significantly reducing the amount of meat in our diets and endeavoring to find at least some substitutes for the animal products we wear or, even better, deciding to cut out meat altogether and to buy only items of clothing that are not made from animal hides or other aspects of animals. A decision to become a vegan, and not just a vegetarian—or at any rate a highly selective purchaser of food—can go even further in the direction of protesting and helping to call attention to and prevent unnecessary or indefensible human-caused animal suffering and deprivation by refraining from buying or eating eggs, milk, and cheese produced in factory farms.

Approximations to final goals matter greatly, both personally and in terms of their social and economic effects. If we find ourselves initially unable to go all the way toward the goals set out in this chapter, beginning to go at least part of the way toward their attainment is a worthy step. Changing the habits of a lifetime may not be, and is usually anything but, easy. Yet it is possible to make such changes over time, to the point where old habits are set aside and new ones become entrenched. What was formerly seen as inordinately difficult to achieve at one time and may even have seemed constitutionally impossible becomes natural, familiar, and second-natured at another.

In this chapter and the previous one, I have argued that sport hunting and fishing and human practices of eating and wearing are critical areas of concern for Religion of Nature, for other religious outlooks and traditions intent upon giving due consideration to the rights and well-being of nonhuman animals—especially those capable of sentience—and for persons, groups, and institutions who do not restrict the focus of morality to human beings and their relationships but include nonhuman animals as well in the scope of much needed and much deserved moral considerability and care. The next chapter is devoted to discussion of some other important ways in which issues relating to the welfare of the nonhuman thous of nature are raised and brought to the fore by human practices in today's world.

6

Other Areas of
Responsibility and Concern

The difficulty in our relation with the animals comes from the sense of *use* as our primary relation with the world around us. Hardly any other attitude so betrays ourselves and the entire universe in which we live. Every being exists in intimate relation with other beings and in a constant exchange of gifts to each other. But this relation is something beyond pragmatic *use*. It is rather a mutual sharing of existence in the grand venture of the universe itself.

—Thomas Berry[1]

Introduction

Cultural historian, student of world religions, and ecological writer Thomas Berry sums up in this chapter's epigraph two fundamental themes of Religion of Nature—themes that are the backbone of this book. The first theme is that nonhuman animals do not exist only for our use any more than we exist only for their use. Our proper relations with them or at least with those of them capable of some degree of conscious awareness are sharing relations of subjects with subjects, not those of human subjects entitled to exploit for their sole benefit hosts of other living beings as mere manipulable objects or automata. We live with these multiple and diverse nonhuman subjects here on earth, as Berry says, in a vast, interdependent community that extends far beyond the community of human beings. And we should aspire to live realistically, responsibly, and thankfully in ways that honor and give utmost recognition to this unalterable fact. To change the metaphor of community to the even more intimate one of family, creatures of earth are our kith and kin, and we should neither ignore nor violate the obligations we have to them as members of the worldwide family to which we all belong.

The second theme brought into prominence by Berry is that our lives as humans together with the lives of the other creatures of earth are but a tiny part of the "grand venture" of the universe as a whole, an adventure stretching back more than thirteen billion years into the past according to contemporary scientific thought and continuing its inexorable changes and developments up to the present moment. Thus, not only can we be filled with a sense of gratitude and wonder by the marvelous diversity of creatures—many of them mentally aware as we are, at least in some degree—with whom we live in mutually dependent community on earth. We can also reflect with reverence and amazement on the majesty of the universe as a whole, with its accelerating cosmic expansion, its distant galaxies, its hundreds of billions of stars within those galaxies coming into being and passing away, its countless planets and their satellites, its restless processes of creation and destruction, its highly probable innumerable forms of emergent life throughout the reaches of space, and its sheer inexplicable givenness.

All of this, stupendous and unimaginable as it is, is not yet to make mention of the distinct possibility that there have been other universes prior to this one, and that there will be still others long after the present one has faded away. According to some cosmologists, many universes other than our own may exist right now and at any other given time. Thus, the story of human life in its relations to other forms of life here on earth; the narrative of this universe's fiery origins, sweeping changes, and eventual entropic demise; the likely tale of the emergence of myriad forms of life from nonlife throughout the universe and not just here on earth; and the possibility of innumerable universes different from our own combine to form a truly spectacular saga—only a few of the chapters of which are known or can be known by us. If these reflections are not sufficient to awaken searching feelings of reverence, astonishment, and awe, what could possibly be? Grand venture indeed!

Am I recommending that we become nature worshippers, then? And am I insisting that this stance is a necessary part of our being concerned with the well-being of animals on earth? In answer to the first question, *worship* is not the right word to use in talking about Religion of Nature. It would be an appropriate response to a personal deity or deities, but nature is not a personal being. One can be committed to nature as religiously ultimate; meditate on nature and one's place in nature and responsibilities to it; discover and create powerful symbols and rituals to explore, express, enact, and share one's commitment;[2] put one's commitment into various forms of appropriate individual and social practice; and find in nature profound challenge, assurance, succor, and meaning. But nature as I conceive it is not a fit object of worship.

As for the second question, I do think that Religion of Nature can provide a highly suitable context and motivation for acknowledging and acting upon our intimate relations with and responsibilities to the other thous of this earth. However, I do not want to suggest or assert that it is the only religious outlook equipped for this purpose. This book is in the main an attempt to spell out the responsibilities to nonhuman animals that flow from the overall vision of Religion of Nature, a vision that centers exclusively on nature and the creatures of nature. It seeks to do so in the context of the haunting beauty, daunting sublimity, and evocative sacredness of the whole of nature, which I am claiming to be in and of itself an appropriate focus of ultimate commitment and concern.

But as I have briefly indicated in the preceding discussions, many other religious outlooks have ample resources from which to draw in developing and proclaiming similar attitudes toward animals to the ones being set forth here. The marvels of nature may not be for some of these religions that which is *most* ultimate and *most* marvelous, but they are generally regarded in these traditions as impressively and superbly marvelous nonetheless. The earth and its creatures may sing the praises of the Lord, as in the Hebrew Psalms, but they do so by being the splendid things the Lord has created them to be. The various religions' respective visions of nature, then, can help to provide context and motivation for their own articulations of our relations and responsibilities as humans to the nonhuman thous of nature.

There is much potential as well as actual common ground among the world's religions in this regard. Religion and morality can and should work together to help bring about direly needed alterations and improvements in the ways we humans relate to the other members of the community of creatures on earth. Much of what I am emphasizing and arguing for in the name of Religion of Nature can also be highlighted and defended on the basis of other religious outlooks. However, I do not presume to speak directly for them here but only for the outlook of Religion of Nature.

So far in this book, I have discussed at some length four major areas of concern that relate to our treatments and mistreatments of nonhuman animals: sport hunting and fishing, farming of animals (especially factory farming[3]), and commercial fishing (especially heavily industrialized techniques of fishing). In this chapter I want to indicate some other areas that call for our moral and religious attention. Much has been written about these areas, but I want to touch briefly on each of them, since they fall squarely within the moral and religious focus of this book. Each of the topics involves momentous consequences for the thous of nature, including but by no means restricted to us human thous. The areas of concern are as follows: animal experimentation; zoos, aquariums, circuses, and rodeos; endangered species and despoliations of natural environments; an exponentially growing human population; and global climate change.

Experimenting on Animals

Nonhuman animals are subjected to many types of experimentation that inflict pain and often repeated pain on them, invade their bodies, alter their genetic makeup, radically restrict and inhibit their normal ways of life, subject them to intense stress and anxiety, and bring about their deaths in massive numbers. Paul Waldau places the number of nonhuman animals used in research worldwide as "in the range of 100–200 million animals annually."[4] These experiments are carried out in the names of applied research, pure research, and education.

The *applied* research experiments are usually justified on the ground that it is necessary to test potential medical and other products (such as cosmetics and food dyes) on animals in order to ensure that they do not bring harm to humans and can be of benefit to them. These experiments can involve deliberately inflicting diseases, and sometimes severely debilitating or fatal diseases, on animals in order repeatedly to test various putative cures for the diseases on the animals, in the hope of developing cures to be used for treatments on human beings. In all such cases, the welfare of nonhuman animals is subordinated to the welfare of humans, and whatever rights the nonhuman animals may be presumed to have are routinely overridden in the interest of contributing to the enhancement of human rights and human well-being.

Thus, what may appear to the unprejudiced eye as a serious conflict of goods—the good of the nonhuman animals in comparison with the good of the human ones—is often dismissed, whether consciously or unconsciously, as a conflict of negligible importance. It tends to be taken for granted that nonhuman forms of life are subordinate to human ones and that in all cases of possible or actual conflict, human interests and needs, including the reduction, elimination, or avoidance of human suffering and pain but often even matters of general and sometimes relatively trivial human convenience, must trump the interests and needs of nonhuman animals. However, as we shall see, the moral and religious issues raised by applied researches involving animals cannot be so easily resolved or set aside.

The *pure* research experiments are conducted for the announced sake of increasing scientific knowledge of physiological functions and for gaining insight into psychological and behavioral functions. These experiments are carried out with no immediate practical applications in mind; their principal aim is increased knowledge and understanding. The experiments are sometimes alarmingly open-ended, haphazard, shot-in-the-dark, and trial-by-error, without well designed hypotheses or exact statistical standards being employed. Bernard Rollin rightly insists that animal research should require extremely careful inquiries into "experimental design, logical coherence, and theoretical groundedness. Atheoretical, 'scatter-gun' empiricism of the sort 'let's see what happens if we try this' sort, without any reason to believe that something *will* happen, is not defensible when the suffering of objects of moral concern is the inevitable result." He discusses behavioral psychology as of the early 1980s as "a paradigm case of bad science and unnecessary cruelty."[5]

As is the case with applied research involving the use of nonhuman animals, the animals in pure research are generally regarded as *models* of human physiology, psychology, and behavior, meaning that knowledge gained through studying them can be assumed to extend, *mutatis mutandis*, to human beings. As models, the nonhuman animals are frequently treated as scientific instruments or as aspects of scientific instrumentation—in other words, as mere tools—with little regard for their character as living beings. Psychologist Kenneth Shapiro makes a strong case for the marked tendency in animal experimentation to reduce an animal "from individual to instrument." And he notes that "some, perhaps most, animal models—this remains an empirical question—are not productive," in the sense of providing significant insights into human disorders or other human factors being modeled. To bolster and illustrate his case, he uses three examples of notably unproductive and inappropriate—but also highly invasive and painful—uses of putative animal models for research into the human eating disorders of bulimia and anorexia. Shapiro therefore pleads for more deliberate and detailed examinations in animal model studies into the assumed but frequently unexamined "hypothesis of similarity."[6]

The conception of nonhuman animals as experimental "models" of human traits, functions, structures, disorders, needs, or modes of behavior strongly implies that the animals are being used as mere means to human ends. Failure to examine carefully the extent to which they can even serve as productive or usable models, given the significant disanalogies as well as analogies between various types of nonhuman animals in comparison to human ones, only adds to the seeming indifference to the former's well-being. The distinctive feelings and needs of nonhuman animals tend to be disregarded unless they have some direct bearing on the search for scientific knowledge. And their lives are routinely terminated as required by the experiments or when, after having being bred or procured for the purpose of experimentation—sometimes in shamefully wasteful numbers—they are deemed to be no longer useful or needed. The prospects of federal protection in the United States for the animals involved in applied and pure research, as well as other areas where treatments of nonhuman animals are concerned, were significantly weakened by the 2002 amendment to the Animal Welfare Act that expressly excluded mice, rats, and birds from the definition of "animal" in that Act.

Much if not most of the animal experiments and procedures that have commonly been used in *education* at the high school, college and university, and graduate school levels—including medical, veterinary, and biological graduate levels—are now superfluous, even though they continue to be employed. There is no need to dissect real animals in biology classes, for example, since educationally effective dissection simulations are available in computer programs. And standard surgical procedures can be effectively communicated in videos or simulated by other artificial means. The communication and illustration of *established* knowledge and procedures can now largely be done, in other words, without having to make use of live animals or even of animals specially killed in enormous numbers for this purpose. There is no need to endlessly replicate this knowledge or these procedures by inflicting pain, suffering, deprivation, or loss of life on conscious beings. At the very least, live animals or animal carcasses should be used for communicating or inculcating these matters only in those special cases where there may be no effective substitute currently conceivable or available. And every effort should be expended to find increasing numbers of such substitutes for use in education. These points would seem to be moral and religious "no-brainers."

But to return to applied and pure research procedures that involve nonhuman animals, the central moral problem raised by them is the conflict of goods between nonhuman and human animals. We have noted that this conflict, on the relatively rare occasions when it is explicitly recognized and dealt with, tends usually to be more or less unquestionably resolved in favor of humans. There are occasions when it admittedly should be resolved in this way, in my judgment. These occasions are those in which significant breakthroughs in understanding and treatment of diseases take place or can reasonably be expected to take place by the use of animals in research. Many lives can be saved as a result, and nonhuman animal lives can sometimes be included in their number. Rather than thinking about this matter in terms of either a blanket defense of animal experimentation or wholesale indictment of all instances of it on the ground of supposed speciesism, it should be thought about on a case-by-case basis, with each of the presumptive rights of nonhuman animals kept always fully in view.

Also, it is legitimate to include in these deliberations questions about the comparative qualities of lives involved. To experiment at present on as small a number of laboratory mice as possible, and without exposing them to unnecessarily invasive, painful, or repeated procedures, in order to help save a large number of human beings from the stress, debilitation, and threat to life of a disease for the indefinite future, would seem to be morally and religiously justifiable.

It is so, not only because of the comparative *numbers* of life-forms involved, both in the present and the future, but also because of the comparative *quality* of a normal human life as compared with that of a mouse. We can assume, for example, that the mouse does not have as vivid a sense of its past and the prospects for its future as does a human being, or as acutely conscious preferences for reasons to live. Peter Singer, an ardent foe of speciesism (in fact, he coined the term), can nevertheless contend that "[i]t is not arbitrary to hold that the life of a self-aware being, capable of abstract thought, of planning for the future, of complex acts of communication, and so on, is more valuable than the life of a being without these capabilities."[7]

This is not an argument for speciesism, because speciesism requires us to think that in all cases without exception the well-being of humans must take precedence over that of animals, meaning in its most general form that whatever serves the good of humans, even to the extent of humans' mild convenience or relatively minor satisfactions, takes indisputable moral precedence over no matter what amount of pain, stress, anxiety, deprivation, mode of life, or loss of life for nonhuman animals may be at stake. But if being a member of the human species by itself is not a justification for treating animals in any way that might suit our human purposes, carefully weighing the comparative quality of the lives in question may constitute such a justification in particular cases.

I must stress, however, the phrase *in particular cases*, because it is essential that we approach and treat conflicts between human and nonhuman goods on a case-by-case basis. There is no general algorithm or rule that can cover all conceivable cases, and it would be a grave moral mistake to think that there is or can be such. We should avoid such abstractions in our deliberations about the comparative well-being of humans and nonhumans, and about how to keep these two forms of well-being in as much moral and religious balance as possible, with full attention to particular cases or types of cases. In no event should we be flagrantly indifferent to or dismissive of the sufferings or the overriding of rights of animals involved in the pursuit of human ends. Instead, we should seek in every way possible to minimize those sufferings and infringements on rights, to find ways to substitute for them whenever possible with technical and artificial means, and to be deeply sensitive to and unfailingly opposed to the plight of animals brought about by careless, needless, poorly designed, unnecessarily repetitive, or unfeeling experimental and educational procedures conducted at their expense. No adequate moral or religious sensibility can think otherwise.

Rodeos, Circuses, Zoos, and Aquariums

Four areas in which the treatments of animals can be matters of grave moral and religious concern are those of rodeos, circuses, zoos, and aquariums. I take brief note of each of these areas in this section, beginning with rodeos.

1. *Rodeos* involve such prominent events as calf roping (or tie-down roping), bronco or bull bucking, and steer wrestling (or bulldogging). These events can inflict severe anxiety, trauma, and injury, and sometimes immediate or early death, on animals for no other reason than the entertainment of the human beings who participate in or observe them. Calves charge out of chutes at full speed (up to 25 or more miles per hour) because they are kicked, have their tails twisted, have their heads knocked, or are prodded with electric shocks. A pursuing rider then ropes the calf, jerking it by its neck to a sudden stop. The rider leaps from the horse and slams the calf onto the ground as he or she proceeds to tie three of its feet together. The event is precisely timed, so all of these procedures take place in the briefest time possible. The calves may sometimes have their legs fractured, their tracheas torn, their internal organs ruptured, or their necks broken. While the crowd cheers, the young animal suffers unimaginable fear, distress, and pain.

The bucking of broncos or bulls is induced by the notorious flank strap, which is cinched with extreme tightness below the animal's rib cage, causing it such pain and distress as to make it buck wildly until the strap is removed. The challenge for the rider is to stay on as long as he or she can before being bucked off. This is also a timed event. The bucking can be exacerbated by spurs worn by the rider, but mostly in a stylized manner with dull spurs and freely rotating rowels meant to imitate the old-time practice of breaking horses by spurring them to buck. The painfully constricting flank strap and induced bucking are hardly enjoyed by the horse or bull, which may have to endure them several times during the time of the rodeo, although they offer excitement to the crowd and challenge and notice to the riders. Human amusement and use are allowed to take precedence over the pain and suffering that must be endured by the nonhuman animals in order to provide it.

Steer wrestling requires one horse rider to keep a steer running in a straight line, while another rider leaps from a horse, grabs the animal by its horns while it is running, and wrestles it to a stop by digging the rider's heels in the ground and twisting the animal's neck around by its horns and nose until it is felled and subdued. The pursuit and the attack are alarming to the animal and run the risk of inflicting serious injury on it. It is an exciting event for the audience, requiring a usually hefty and always impressively courageous cowboy to wrestle a 450 to 650 pound steer to the ground. Quick action and exact technique are required. The event is timed and quickly concluded. There is no way of describing the event, however, as an act of kindness to the animal concerned. It is shunted into an arena full of screaming fans, guided or pursued by fast-riding horsemen, abruptly stopped in its tracks, its horns grabbed and head wrenched painfully around, and its massive body plumped onto the ground.

There is a running dispute between animal welfare agencies and activists, on the one hand, and defenders of rodeos as wholesome family entertainment, on the other, about how much risk there is to the animals involved in such events or how much actual injury to them takes place. Defenders can argue, for example, that it is now commonplace for veterinarians to be in attendance at many rodeos to give prompt medical care to the animals if needed, and that many regulations now in force effectively prevent cruel treatments of animals. But we need to take note of the fact that little benefit, if any, accrues to the nonhuman animals from their participation in rodeos and to weigh carefully the question of whether the risks they encounter or actual sufferings and injuries they are forced to endure can be justified. It is sometimes argued that there is considerable risk of injury to the human participants in rodeos too, especially in precarious events such as steer wrestling. But the human participants take the risks willingly, and they have a choice in the matter, whereas the nonhuman ones do not.

Measures to monitor the treatment and welfare of the animals and the passage of laws or enactment of regulations to mitigate the risks of their injury are welcome, of course, but there would seem to be no compelling reason to allow these traditional rodeo events, given the anguish, pain, and risks they typically inflict upon animals. As for the notion that rodeos are wholesome family entertainment, we need to ask ourselves whether we wish young people to be taught by example that routine endangerment of or cruelty to of animals simply for the sake of human challenge and entertainment is morally and religiously acceptable.

The cruel or potentially cruel treatments of animals in rodeos such as the ones I have indicated here should be prohibited outright, not just carefully monitored and ameliorated. That being said, the latter course is preferable to the remaining alternative of thoughtless indifference. It can bring immediate benefit to animals even while the struggle for the ideal of complete prohibition goes on. The ever-present potential downside of the ameliorating and compromising approach, however, is that the ultimate goal of ending the practices that endanger the animals in the first place might be lost sight of. The better course of action is preferable to the worst one in the short run, but it cannot substitute indefinitely for the best and most completely satisfactory course—that of avoiding the anxiety, trauma, and danger to the animals by bringing a complete end to the events in question.

2. The treatment of animals in *circuses* is also reprehensible and often brutal. Elephants, for example, are a featured animal in many circuses. They are social animals used to roaming about in large groups. But in circuses they are tethered to the ground by their feet when they are not traveling or performing. They are transported repeatedly in confined quarters. They are trained to do the tricks audiences enjoy by harsh techniques the audiences are never allowed to see. They are hit frequently and furiously with large poles, and pieces of their skin are gouged out with the sharp hooks at the ends of the poles. Electric prods are used on them, and the hair on their skins may be burned off with blow torches. It is common practice for them to be yelled at, cursed, and treated with contempt by trainers and handlers. Being intimidated, dominated, cowed, and hurt is generally regarded as a necessary part of their training and as the only way to keep these huge animals at bay and under control. Elephants young and old are forced by such morally unconscionable and indefensible methods to

perform and live out their lives in a manner entirely contrary to their nature—all for the sake of human amusement.

Other large animals such as lions, tigers, and bears are confined to cages in which they can barely move around, despite the fact that by nature they are inclined to roam over large areas as they hunt or forage. They too, as well as horses, dogs, and other animals, are forced by means such as whips, prods, and other types of intimidation to learn the tricks audiences love to see. They too are transported from city to city in closely confined quarters. When the animals are not performing, they can be observed to be morose and frustrated as they pace back and forth in their cages, totally cut off from their normal modes of life. To witness innocent human beings treated in such sad and reprehensible ways would promote immediate protests from any morally sensitive person. To imagine one's own self being forced to live in this way would be too horrible to contemplate. One would seek to avoid such treatment in any way possible.

Nevertheless, these circus animals are enslaved and imprisoned throughout their lifetimes, as well as being regularly subjected to often brutal methods of domination and control. Do our fellow animals not mutely cry out for our deepest sympathy and for long overdue cessation of the practices that cause and permit their suffering? Is our human entertainment of such great, overriding value as to countenance the plight of these animals? The answer to these questions seems to me to be obvious. I can think of no way in which the practices of animal circuses can be morally or religiously sanctioned, once they are acknowledged and seriously contemplated. The practices betray uncaring indifference to what I have termed the four Rs and are blatant violations of the six presumptive rights of nonhuman animals for which I have argued.

There are of course other ways of thinking; mine is not the only possible or actual perspective. But it is hard for me to imagine a different but still plausible moral or religious lens from which such practices could be tolerated or viewed with equanimity.

3. Keeping animals in *zoos* is generally defended on the ground that it provides important educational value to the public, and especially to children, by acquainting people with the lives, distinctive natures, and appearances of a large number of animals—animals that otherwise might never be seen. Here, it is argued, the animals are well

fed, well treated, and kept safe. Children may have watched some of these animals in the movies or on television, or read about them in books, but never have witnessed them in the flesh. Now they have the opportunity to encounter them in zoos and to be taught, impressed, and awed by their actual presence. How else would they have the opportunity to see such diverse creatures as gorillas, penguins, giraffes, monkeys, kangaroos, tigers, polar bears, and exotic snakes? The animals benefit from their protection and care and the humans do as well, so what could be morally or religiously objectionable in that?

Unfortunately, all is not as it may appear. The animals are captured and torn from their native settings and prohibited from living in ways natural to them. There is little educational value to children or others in observing animals in the artificial zoo environments, so alien to and remote from their natural environments. The animals are enslaved, wholly dominated by humans, and imprisoned in cages, pens, or settings that greatly restrict their normal activities. Their inner lives and distinctive forms of subjective awareness tend generally to be radically downplayed or ignored. They suffer from frustration and boredom. For example, they may pace restlessly and endlessly in their cages, inflict various kinds of injury on themselves, or protestingly spread their feces around where they are penned. These are behavioral signs of stress, monotony, and acute annoyance, indications that the animals are far from being happy or content with their lot. They are gawked at and sometimes made fun of or tormented by visitors to the zoos. Their naturally rich and challenging ways of life in their indigenous environments are reduced to the impoverished role of being helpless pawns of human use, education, and enjoyment.

In zoos animals tend for the most part to be regarded as fascinatingly diverse mobile exhibits put there for exclusively human purposes rather than as intrinsically valuable subjects or thous, the quality of whose psychic lives demands conscientious moral consideration. To routinely imprison, manipulate, restrict, frustrate, and control beings capable in ordinary circumstances of significantly high levels of conscious awareness is a *prima facie* wrong, and it is not at all clear to me that the wrong is overridden by a more compelling right. Zoo animals may not suffer as much in the more obvious physical ways that rodeo or circus animals do, but their often grievous and pitiable psychic sufferings should not be underestimated or overlooked. In the perspective of Religion of Nature, zoos should be phased out as the relic of a less morally and religiously sensitive past, as another sad example of an all too prevalent domineering, uncaring, and cruel human attitude toward other creatures of earth. My hope is that many others will come to view the matter in this way, if they have not done so already, and that actions will be taken in the not too distant future by concerned citizens and courts to phase out and eventually close down public and private zoos. Whatever benefits zoos may be argued to bestow upon humans are heavily outweighed by the wrongs against nonhuman animals they tacitly endorse, teach, and sustain.

4. Much of the argument I have presented against the maintenance of zoos applies also to *aquariums*. To see a magnificent animal such as a dolphin or shark sleekly gliding by an observation port in a tank of sea water in a public aquarium, even while knowing that the animal is protected and well fed, fills me with pity and remorse. I feel the same way when encountering a brightly lit tank of sea water in a place like a restaurant or office building, with exotic tropical fish moving monotonously to and fro, up and down, day after day within the narrow confines of their watery boxes solely for human amusement. Our understandable fascination with being able to view these animals at close range should not be allowed to blind us to the sad effects of their lifelong confinement. We tend to forget or ignore that fact that these are creatures with distinctive natures and with their own kinds of psychic needs, wants, frustrations, enjoyments, possibilities, and fulfillments. To cut them off for no compelling reason from their natural modes of life within their indigenous environments is to inflict great wrong on them. They exist for their own self-contained, self-directed purposes, not merely for ours.

I present and argue for my views in this book in the spirit of ongoing dialogue and in the hope that those who disagree with me will take such views seriously into consideration. The issues I raise are generally complex, controversial, and in need of concerted discussion and analysis, with a view to finding the best resolutions now and in the future for both humans and other living beings. Such disagreements often tend to be pitted against each other in a purely confrontational manner. It is far better that they be acknowledged as starting points for engaged and constructive dialogue. Clear articulation of the starting points and their rationales is an essential part of the process. I offer this book and the presentation and defense of my views in this spirit.

Endangered Species and Despoliations
of Natural Environments

Extinctions of species are anything but rare in earth's history. At least five massive species extinctions have taken place in the past, and more than 99 percent of the total number of earth's evolved species is estimated to have become extinct through natural causes over the course of time. We are in critical danger of another period of massive species extinctions in our own time. Scientist have disagreed over the past decade or so about methods for calculating the rates of extinctions going on at the present time, but almost all of them agree that the rates are matters of serious concern and that they stand in sharp contrast with rates of extinctions prior to the onset of the Industrial Revolution and with average rates characterizing extinctions in the evolutionary time scale of the planet.

Berry argues that the Cenozoic geological era in which we are living is becoming a sixth time of actual and impending massive worldwide extinctions—now largely caused by human beings—and that our only hope of putting an end to these extinctions or slowing them in significant numbers is consciously adapting drastically new attitudes, policies, and practices that can inaugurate what he terms a new "Ecozoic" era. This hoped-for era would be one of profound and newly awakened human sensitivity to and concern for all forms of life on earth and for the preservation or restoration of natural environments in which these diverse ways of life can be safeguarded and allowed to flourish.[8]

The principle factors accounting for the extremely high rate of extinctions today are a burgeoning human population that has reached the seven billion mark and continues to grow at a rapid rate, the encroachments of this population's activities and wastes on the habitats of innumerable species, and its rapidly increasing technological utilizations of energy sources such as coal, oil, and natural gas extractions and uses that pollute the seas, ground, and air and foster a potentially disastrous global climate change through the greenhouse effect. Oil wells are drilled on land and sea. Electric power plants are built and fueled with relatively cheap and abundant but drastically polluting coal. Gasoline or diesel powered automobiles and trucks in increasing numbers spew out their tailpipe emissions throughout the world. Mountains are mined or topped for coal and their debris of heavy metals left to enter into nearby streams and endanger the wildlife that depend on those streams and the bays and seas into which they lead. Wetlands are drained; rivers are dammed; forests are torched or felled; seas are overfished and enormous numbers of bycatches repeatedly destroyed. Land species are overharvested; rare species are poached. Lands are overgrazed, leading to erosion or desertification. Diverse grasslands, meadows, and woods are converted to monocultural farms. Livestock emit the greenhouse gas methane, adding to the threat of global climate change; aquifers and rivers are tapped for city water and agricultural irrigation; invasive species are introduced unwittingly or intentionally; pesticides are widely deployed; wastes in huge amounts and of varied types are produced but not properly disposed of. All such human activities, greatly exacerbated by a rapidly growing human population, threaten the habitats and livelihoods of animals and plants throughout the earth. If not properly recognized, attended to, and brought under control, such activities can result (and already are resulting) in the extinctions of vast numbers of species of living beings and the wiping out of whole ecosystems. It is by now well recognized that a threat to one or just a few species in an ecosystem can pose a threat to all its creatures because of the intricacy of relation among the diverse species in the system.

The connection between human activities and mounting species extinctions can be seen with special clarity in the fact that there is a direct correlation between the increasing human uses of energy over the past two centuries and the expanding rates of animal and plant extinctions in that same period. "By every conceivable measure," writes biologist Edward O. Wilson, "humanity is ecologically abnormal. Our species appropriates between 20 and 40 percent of the solar energy captured in organic material by land plants. There is no way that we can draw upon the resources of the planet to such a degree without drastically reducing the state of most other species."[9] My principle concern in this book is with nonhuman animals, but animals cannot survive apart from an interlinked food chain that critically involves the survival and availability of plant species.

Once a species is gone from the earth, it can never be replaced. What evolution has accomplished over millions of years can be destroyed in a relatively brief span of time by the activities of human beings. The International Union for the Conservation of Nature reported in November of 2011, for example, that *twenty-five percent* of all of the earth's mammals are currently in danger of extinction.[10] If we are at all concerned about our treatments of nonhuman animals and the consequences of our relations with them, we must care deeply about the varied human practices and the encroaching, disruptive, and dislodging presence of cascading numbers of human beings on earth that imperil the survival of irreplaceable species of animals and plants. And we must translate our concern into devising, supporting, and implementing policies that can meet the crisis of endangered species head-on. Our technological prowess has brought us to this crisis. We need now to apply our intelligence, resourcefulness, and resolve to find ways of effectively educating about it, responding to it, and reversing it while we still have time to do so. To do so means, among other things, exposing and fighting against the interests and agencies in our present societies that want to forestall or minimize the importance of such efforts because of short-term, narrowly focused economic or other considerations, because of the influence and grip of alternate views of the world, or because of sheer indifference or neglectful ignorance.

This is no easy battle since it must confront deeply entrenched and strongly influential centers of power in present society and requires astute strategies for comprehending and combating these centers of power. Philosopher Wesley J. Wildman emphasizes this point when he states that "[s]ome of the most urgent practical questions confronting human beings concern how power dynamics work, how they can be regulated, and how they can be turned in just and good directions."[11] Effectively dealing with these questions about the structures and dynamics of power in our attempts to respond to the looming crisis of endangered species is no mean feat, but the magnitude and urgency of the crisis require that we make every effort to do so, especially if we are in sympathy with the spirit and general outlines of the moral and religious outlook being laid out in this book.

There is evidence that species declines can be reversed, but as Richard Edwards, the Chief Executive Officer of Windscreen, insists, in order for this to happen on a significantly large scale "[w]e need to address our disconnection from the natural world, and will only succeed in rescuing species from the brink of extinction, if we successfully communicate their plight, significance, value, and importance." Professor Jonathan Baillie, Director of Conservation Programmes at the ZSL London Zoo, speaks in a similar manner when he contends,

"Fundamentally, it is our values that need to change if we are to avert the looming extinction crisis."[12]

I have mentioned in this section the exponentially growing human population of our time that along with other factors threatens the carrying capacity of the earth and the survival of many of its creatures and their species. I also mentioned here the present looming menace of global climate change that is to a large extent attributable by the most reliable scientific reports to the activities of human beings following upon the Industrial Revolution. In the next section and the one following I want briefly to address these two critically important and closely related topics in more detail, so as to bring into clear focus their immediate and longer range implications for the welfare and survival of the thous of nature, including us human beings. I take up first the human population explosion and then the issue of global climate change.

The Human Population Explosion

Explosion is the right word to use in describing this phenomenon. Population biologist Paul R. Erlich in 1968 published a book called *The Population Bomb*. His title carries the connotation of an explosion or sudden eruption and oppressive encroachment of human population in our time that threatens the quality of life and survival of life-forms and their species throughout the earth and of us humans as well.[13] The dire warnings of Erlich's book have not diminished in their general veracity or force from that date to the present. In 1800, the human population is estimated to have been about one billion persons. By 1920, it was around two billion. The United Nations announced that the world's population of humans on November 1, 2011, had reached seven billion and predicted that, at present rates of growth, it would reach ten billion by the end of the twenty-first century. Since 1960, we humans have been adding a *billion* people every twelve to thirteen years.[14]

Another way to look at this rate of population growth throughout the world is the estimate by Kierán Suckling, Executive Director of the Center for Biological Diversity, that we are adding more than two-hundred thousand people to the earth *every day*. Suckling observes that "[t]he costs of doing nothing about overpopulation are steep and profound. Indeed, they are unacceptable. Left unchecked, the human species is lining up to wipe thousands of other species out of existence. If that happens, this planet will indeed be a very lonely place, left only with the remnants of the wild world this place once was." He also takes note of the crucial fact that "every essential human need depends on the diversity that exists in the natural world."[15] This being the case, the threats to nonhuman forms of life raised by the steepening rates of human population pose severe dangers to the lives and quality of life of human beings as well.

The problem is compounded by the fact that in India, China, and other so-called developing countries even when the birth rate drops, the resulting smaller families tend to consume more as their incomes rise, meaning that "a country's carbon footprint does not necessarily shrink when the birth rate drops."[16] So the greenhouse gas issue and its connection with global climate change, to be discussed in the next section, is a function of the rate of human consumption and not just of the rate of population growth, although the two are closely connected.

Significant sources of the worldwide population explosion include greatly improved medical technology, with its lowering of child mortality, more effective means of preventing and curing diseases, and extension of age limits; and greater efficiency in the production and distribution of food. But another important source is the low use or absence of effective birth control methods, due to such factors as negligence, ignorance, religious and other cultural prohibitions, and relatively high costs or limited availability—at least in some areas of the world—of birth control techniques such as the ordinary condom. Making knowledge of birth control techniques more widely available and distributing the means for avoiding pregnancies in areas where these are not easily affordable or available is an important contribution to reducing the rate of population growth throughout the world.

Persuading people to make regular use of these techniques is a formidable task, however. Even in the United States, where we would assume that the relevant knowledge is widespread and the birth control techniques are readily available, unintended pregnancies account for roughly half of the annual births, according to studies by the Guttmacher Institute in New York City.[17] Moreover, Erlich is surely correct in noting that family planning alone is not sufficient to stem unbridled population growth, and that a fundamental change of *attitudes* relating to our role as humans in nature is a crucial requirement.[18] The pressing need for radical change in current basic attitudes, values, and their accompanying practices—especially in the areas of morality and religion—is what the present book is emphasizing, not only as it affects the present wildfire rates of human population growth and their devastating impacts on nonhuman creatures, but as it affects all of the ways in which we regard and relate to our fellow creatures. Another threat of major significance that looms over the earth and its various life-forms today is global climate change, and effective responses to this threat will also require fundamental changes of outlook, value assessment, commitment, and practice on the part of human beings.

The Threat of Global Climate Change

The flora and fauna of the earth are faced today with the grim threat of global climate change. This change is due to a sizeable extent to the activities of human beings following upon the Industrial Revolution, and is the effect primarily, although not exclusively, of the widespread burning of coal to fuel power plants and other industries. Airplanes, automobiles, and livestock also contribute, as do other factors. Associated Press science writer Seth Borenstein reported on November 3, 2011, that the world pumped about 564 million more metric tons of carbon into the air in 2010 than it did in 2009, resulting in an increase of six percent. This means that the global output of heat-trapping carbon increased by the largest amount on record in 2010, according to calculations of the United States Department of Energy. While the developed countries that ratified the 1997 Kyoto Protocol (it is notable that the United States did not) have reduced their overall emissions, the developing ones such as China and India continue to increase theirs as they become more industrialized and economically prosperous. China, India, and the United States are today the top producers of greenhouse gasses.[19]

The impacts of global warming are now readily apparent in the Arctic, for example, where temperatures have arisen and ice is melting, both at an alarming rate. The Arctic is warming twice as fast as other parts of the world: the temperature in Alaska, for example, increasing 5.4 degrees Fahrenheit between 1970 and 2000.[20] For the first time in recollectable history, the famed Northwest Passage at the top of the North American continent is navigable by oceangoing vessels because of the sudden radical diminution and thinning of sea ice. Shrinking polar bear habitat is another consequence. There is a perilous feedback process operating here. Less white ice means less albedo or reflecting of the sun's rays back into the atmosphere, and thus more absorption of heat by the earth and seas. As permafrost bogs are melted in the far north, methane is released into the atmosphere. Methane is a greenhouse gas that reflects heat back onto the earth. So one process feeds into and reinforces the other. Since 1947, the Antarctic Peninsula, in the extreme south of the earth, has warmed an average of 4.5 degrees Fahrenheit, and the Southern Ocean is warming as well. Krill that are the major food source for seals, whales, and penguins in the Antarctic, feed on algae found on sea ice. With the decrease in sea ice, they have declined 80 percent since the 1970s.[21]

The melting of ice in the two polar areas also raises the levels of the seas, and this rise in water level threatens the survival of species of fish and other aquatic animals inhabiting the wetlands and shores of the continents and islands. Melting ice also adds fresh water to the seas, and the greenhouse effect warms the oceans. Salinity and water temperature are affected, adding to the danger of extinctions to many life-forms in the sea, finely attuned and adapted as they are to precise levels of temperature and salinity. Increased carbon dioxide in the atmosphere that is caused by high rates of fossil burning, when absorbed by the seas, increases the seas' acidity. Food chains can be drastically affected by these factors. Warmer water in the Atlantic affects the flow of the Gulf Stream, which is dependent on present gradients of temperatures in the ocean, and has the potential to change the climate of the United Kingdom and other north Atlantic areas, making them significantly colder. This factor too affects flora and fauna in the sea and on land in this region of the world.

The warming of the land and air around the world, largely attributable to the burning of fossil fuels by humans, affects the habitats of land animals and plants, driving them toward higher latitudes or altitudes. It increases the temperature of formerly cooler locales, and makes even hotter those that were already hot. Drought and desertification in some areas and severe storms and floods in others can result from the alterations of temperature. Some species of animals and plants may not be able to adapt to the changes quickly enough, and they may become extinct. Whole ecosystems can be affected in this way. A report of the National Wildlife Federation sums up the consequences of global climate change for nonhuman life-forms in this way: "Species may not be able to adapt to this rapid climate change or to move fast enough to more suitable areas as their current areas become less suitable for them. Unless significant action is taken now, global warming will likely become the single most important factor to affect wildlife since the emergence of mankind."[22]

So once again and in yet another way, the activities of the earth's human thous are now having, and threatening imminently to have, destructive and disastrous effects on the well-being of the nonhuman ones. Radical reexaminations of and fundamental, far-reaching changes in our human attitudes and practices are urgently called for. We owe these reexaminations and changes to our fellow creatures as well as to ourselves. We are critically dependent on them, as they are on us. Compassionate, knowledgeable, and vigilant morality and religion call out for basic rethinkings and revisions of many current human outlooks and practices, for our own sake as well as for the sake of the innumerable other forms of life and their distinctive species on earth.

In this chapter and in Chapter 5, I discussed a variety of areas in which this fundamental rethinking and revision needs to take place. Some of these areas, such as sport hunting and fishing, factory farming and industrial fishing, rodeos, circuses, zoos, and aquariums, and animal experimentations affect a relatively specific, smaller, but still highly significant number of animals capable of sentience. Other areas, such as those of endangered species and widespread despoliations of natural environments, the human population explosion, and global climate change have more massive and far-reaching implications for these animals and their species and ecosystems across the globe. But each of the areas is important, and within them, as we have seen, treatments of nonhuman animals by us humans and the effects of our actions on them—whether intentional or non-intentional—are matters of imperative moral and religious concern.

In the seventh and final chapter of this book, I shall respond to some major objections to the outlooks and practices I am endorsing and recommending. I want there also to address more explicitly the critical issue of the sources of *empowerment* in Religion of Nature. This aspect of Religion of Nature and its two other basic aspects of *assurance* and *demand* were mentioned in Chapter 1.[23] The assurance aspect was given some prominence in discussion of the fourth R in

Chapter 3, but the empowerment aspect was again only mentioned there. The demand aspect has been pervasive through all the previous chapters. In the last part of the concluding chapter I shall present a set of basic principles and injunctions as a way of highlighting and summarizing the central observations and arguments of the book.

7

A New Moral and Religious Consciousness

. . . [T]hough I'm a secular person and a scientist, I believe that our relationship with the living world must be mainly religious. But I don't mean theological. I mean religious in the sense of reverent, revolutionary, spiritual, and inspired. Reverent because the world is unique, thus holy. Revolutionary in making a break with the drift and downdraft of outdated, maladaptive modes of thought. Spiritual in seeking attainment of a higher realm of human being. Inspired in the aspiration to connect crucial truths with wider communities. Religious in precisely this way: connection, with a sense of purpose.

—Carl Safina[1]

Introduction

It is regrettable that we in the West have for so long had an instinctive and unanalyzed tendency to identify the word *religion* with belief in God, thus blinding ourselves to the facts that there are many religions of the world which are not monotheistic and that it is possible to be deeply religious without believing in God. Naturalist and marine biologist Carl Safina, author of the words I am using as the epigraph for this chapter, professes in his book *The View from Lazy Point* to be "a secular person and a scientist," but by "secular" he apparently means "non-theist." The epigraph and the book from which it is taken are permeated with profound religious sensibility as well as acute moral concern both in their celebrations of the wondrous diversity and multiple ways of life of nonhuman animals, and in their warnings about the ominous plights and endangerments of these animals and their species in the contemporary world.[2]

Safina's pervasive religious sensibility and passionate moral concern are thus tightly interwoven, each informing the other. The moral concern provides the necessary outlet, expression, and response for the deep-lying religious sensibility, while the religious sensibility opens up an expansive and inspiring vision of the numinous world of which we humans are a part and for whose continuing well-being we have special responsibility. This special responsibility may not be a gift of God, as it is not in Safina's perspective nor in that of Religion of Nature, but it flows from our manifest human ability—by virtue of our intellectual capacities and technological competencies—either to do considerable harm to the other creatures of nature or to make substantial contributions to their protection and support. Safina's phrase "connection with a sense of purpose" nicely captures the conjoining of religion and morality, and the indispensable importance each has for the other, so far as our attitudes and practices in relation to nonhuman animals and their environments are concerned.

As I mentioned toward the end of the previous chapter, in the present chapter I want to do three things. The first is to flesh out the critical notion of *empowerment* in Religion of Nature as it bears particularly on the changes of attitude and practice in relation to nonhuman animals I am calling for and urging to be considered. The second is to present and respond to several major objections to the arguments and claims, outlooks, and positions I have developed to this point. The third is to set out some summary observations and exhortations that constitute the central themes of this book. I turn first, then, to the notion of empowerment.

Empowerment in Religion of Nature

It has often been noted that there is a distinction between the priestly (assuring, supportive, conserving, enabling) and prophetic (demanding, critical, innovative, revolutionary) functions of religious traditions.

Psalm 34: 9 in the Hebrew Bible reads, "O consider and see that the Lord is good; / Happy is the man that taketh refuge in Him." And Psalm 145: 17–19 states, "The Lord is righteous in all His ways, / And gracious in all His works. / The Lord is nigh unto all them that call upon Him, / To all that call upon Him in truth. / He will fulfill the desire of them that fear Him; / He will also hear their cry, and will save them."[3] These are eloquent statements of the assurance function. In the book of Amos, on the other hand, we find these words spoken by a wrathful God, "I hate, I despise your feasts, / And I will take no delight in your solemn assemblies. / Yea, though ye offer me burnt-offerings and your meal-offerings, I will not accept them; / Neither will I regard the peace-offerings of your fat beasts. / Take away from Me the noise of thy songs; / And let Me not hear the melody of thy psalteries. / But let justice well up as waters, / And righteousness as a mighty stream."[4] Here the fiery prophet speaking in the name of the Lord inveighs against complacent preoccupation with priestly ceremonies and conventions and focuses attention on the pressing demand for justice and righteousness. In the present book, I have laid great stress on the prophetic function of Religion of Nature in its relations to nonhuman animals as I view that function, but we should not lose sight of the more priestly functions of assurance and empowerment.

In fighting for the rights and welfare of nonhuman animals, we are not, in the perspective of Religion of Nature, fighting on behalf of alien creatures belonging to another world, but for fellow creatures of one and the same world. Salvation in the perspective of Religion of Nature is not restricted to humans but applies to nonhumans as well. It consists in the continuing protection, betterment, and flourishing of the world as a whole here and now, not in the hope of being transported beyond this finite, fragile, vulnerable world into some other realm, allegedly forever secure from frustration, struggle, disappointment, and loss. We and all our fellow creatures are not only *on* the earth but *of* the earth. We belong nowhere else, and we inhabit the earth in tightly woven webs of interdependence. We share in our earthly life's sustenance and protection, but also in its uncertainties and dangers.

There is no transcendent, supernatural Thou to whom we humans can appeal for guidance and help, but we can make use of the remarkable resources nature has implanted in us and derive constant inspiration and motivation from nature's numinous presence and power.

Furthermore, nature itself as I am portraying it here is not blank, brute, and unfeeling—with ourselves as the sole exceptions to its bleakly impersonal character—but is filled with conscious beings akin to us in many ways. We humans have the privilege and responsibility of drawing upon our distinctive natural gifts to protect the integrity, beauty, diversity, and providingness of the earth and its creatures. There is quiet *assurance* in this task and daunting *demand* as well. But in the grip of this vision, there is also a strong sense of *empowerment*. We have a crucial role to play in the world and can be grateful that this is so. Humbled and moved by the awesome mystery and sacredness of nature to which we miraculously belong, we can be inspired to become caring, compassionate, responsible members of the community of creatures on earth. Sensitive, responsive awareness of our membership in this community can itself be tremendously empowering.

This larger community of nature of which we are a part and to which we are responsible gives meaning to our individual lives as well as motivating and inspiring our contributions to the community as a whole. To *manipulate* the world and its creatures and to think of ourselves as warranted to manipulate them to suit our own whims, desires, and presumed needs—as we typically have done in the past and in many ways sadly continue to do in the present—is to be radically *alienated* from the world. Such attitudes and practices also alienate us from ourselves, blinding us to our true nature as natural beings living in crucial dependence upon other aspects of the natural world.

The caring, compassionate attitude toward our fellow creatures I am urging throughout this book is antithetical to manipulation of them and can create in us a healing and ennobling sense of community and belonging. For us humans to feel at home in the world is to be empowered to live in it with confidence and joy, and to be instinctively disposed to contribute what we can *to it* instead of merely taking *from it*. What Zen Buddhist David Loy says about our relationship to the human community applies also to our relationship to the wider community of nonhuman forms of life:

> The delusion of separation becomes wisdom when we realize that no one is an island. We are interdependent because we are all part of each other, different facets of the same jewel we call the earth. The world is not a collection of objects but a community of subjects, a web of interacting

processes. Our 'interpenetration' means that we cannot avoid responsibility for each other.[5]

To have such responsibility for all the creatures of earth is to be given a vital role to play in the world. This sense of responsibility and demand can awaken in us an inherent, upwelling power to meet the responsibility and demand, namely, the power of *love*.

Following an insightful suggestion of Loy,[6] the three aspects of assurance, demand, and empowerment I have associated with Religion of Nature and, in fact, with religious outlooks in general, are when taken together another way of speaking of love. Love is a reciprocal relation, implying both gracious care and concern for the beloved and also welcoming acceptance of the grace of being loved in return. Does nature love us? It does, at least metaphorically, in the senses of providing us with the varied means necessary for our sustenance, creativity, and flourishing; admitting us into its larger community of an amazing array of life-forms, similar to us in many important ways but also astoundingly different from us in other ways; enabling us to be keenly conscious of the world and of ourselves as parts of the world; giving us crucial responsibility to the community of earth's creatures; bestowing on us distinctive capacities for relating positively and helpfully to this community; and surrounding and suffusing us with nature's overwhelming beauty and sublimity. The marvel and inspiration of each of these gifts of nature, when rightly recognized and responded to, are magnificently empowering. *And nothing is more deeply and lastingly empowering than the giving and receiving of love.* In the final analysis, this book and all that it stands for can be regarded as a hymn to love, to the cherishing of creatures different from ourselves and to instilling the driving spirit of that cherishing into our everyday outlooks and practices.

Such love can be transformative for us and for the nature of which we are a part. It will neither save us from eventual death, nor take us to heaven when we die; nor will it insulate us from the struggles, perils, uncertainties, and tragedies of our finite existence—an existence we share with all other living beings. But by removing an arrogant, manipulative, misconceived, destructive focus exclusively on ourselves, this love can help to save us and our fellow creatures from an earthly hell of our own making. It can inspire us to envision and incorporate into our lives acknowledgment of our togetherness with all of the earth's creatures and of the distinctive contributions we humans can make and must increasingly learn how to make to the maintenance and defense of our common terrestrial home.

In other words, there are latent resources in us as individuals and in our progressively learning how effectively to plan and work with our fellow human beings for the good of nature that can be activated by a captivating vision of the sacredness of nature and of our shared destiny and potential loving relationship with all the types of living beings inhabiting it. "Biophilia" is not in the final analysis an alien, unnatural, contrived attitude that must be imposed on us from without but a sentiment that lies dormant and ready to be awakened within each of us.[7] With its awakening and enlivening can come steady strengthening of the transformative power required to do its bidding. This conviction is a basic theme of Religion of Nature and is central to its concept of empowerment.

Objections and Replies

In this section I am going to anticipate four major objections to key aspects of the moral and religious attitudes and practices I am convinced we humans should work toward in our relations to the nonhuman thous of nature. I shall present each of the objections in turn and state my responses to it. In this way, I can clarify further the rationale for some of the aims, values, and recommendations of the book and show in more detail how they can be defended.

1. The first objection is that predictable effects on our nation's and the world's economy of the radical outlooks, practices, and changes I am recommending make their implementations both highly unlikely and extremely undesirable. For example, a large-scale reduction or end to sport hunting and fishing would severely affect the purchase of hunting and fishing licenses on which the oversight and maintenance of parks, waterways, and their wildlife depend, and it would have damaging effects on those aspects of the economy that provide clothing, supplies, and employment for these popular activities. Putting an end to factory farming and industrial fishing would mean giving up the far greater economic efficiency provided by these industries, as well as the loss of a substantial number of jobs.

Closing down rodeos, circuses, zoos, and aquariums would mean losing the jobs, fees, and other economic benefits connected with these enterprises. Greatly reducing or ending the consumption of meat would have devastating effects that would ripple through the established economies of farms, fisheries, cities, nations, and the world. The costs and enormous changes to industries and the economy of trying to find and establish affordable, efficient, renewable alternative sources of energy and finally of bringing to an end fossil fuel utilization are too staggering to contemplate. As long as coal is cheap and plentiful, we should not expect that its use as fuel will be abandoned or even significantly reduced, especially in poorer countries that possess coal in abundance or where it is readily available through trade. Economically feasible substitutes for oil and natural gas are nowhere in sight. Finally, animal experimentation is necessary, not only to diagnose and prevent or even eliminate human diseases, but also to ensure that products are not harmful to human beings—and to avoid heavy economic penalties if they should prove to be so.

My responses to this economic line of objection are as follows. With regard to sport hunting and fishing, I am not arguing that these should be brought to an end by legal enactments but only urging that individual hunters and fishers should carefully consider the moral and religious implications of their practices and ask themselves whether wounding, traumatizing, and killing animals when not needed for food, solely for entertainment, or even for alleged spiritual edification is morally defensible. Rodeos, animal circuses, zoos, and aquariums should eventually be prohibited by law for the reasons I have given. Rodeos, for example, are already legally banned in such places as Great Britain, The Netherlands, and the city of Vancouver in the Canadian Province of British Columbia. Avoiding cruelty to animals in these four enterprises outweighs whatever benefits in entertainment, education, or economics they are claimed to provide.

As for ending or greatly reducing the consumption of meat, although I have given economic, ecological, and moral reasons for thinking that this is a commendable idea, I am not naïve enough to think that it can or should be implemented overnight. I am also fully aware that strict vegetarianism is and should remain a matter of personal choice, not legal enactment, and I do not want to be thought arrogant or confrontational when proposing what I consider to be plausible reasons in its defense. I do, however, want to share, and share as forcibly and persuasively as I can, my moral and religious reflections concerning the eating of animals. I am also well aware of the gigantic turnaround in the allocation of economic resources any large-scale reduction of the consumption of meat would require. The basic thrust of my argument regarding the issue of eating of animals is that consumption of meat should not for a moment allow mistreatment in the rearing and handling of animals, and though it does require that animals be slaughtered, that they should be slaughtered in the most humane and painless ways possible. Care for animals should be the watchword throughout, not mere economic efficiency if we are to take seriously the moral and religious outlook and commitment elaborated and supported in this book.

Even if there are losses in economic efficiency by radically altering or eliminating the present forms of factory farming and industrial fishing, the tradeoff in more humane treatment of animals is morally and religiously worth it. Economic considerations should not be allowed to sanction cruelty to animals under any circumstances.[8] Producers of food products from the land and the sea should be responsibly regulated by government agencies and their own internal oversight agencies in accordance with this principle, and consumers must be willing to pay the possible higher costs of less efficient but more humane (and sustainable) food production. They must also be given reliable information about farming and fishing modes of production to ensure that when they do opt to purchase food with the treatment of animals as an important concern, they can trust the labeling and other sources of that information.[9] Similar reasoning applies, as I have shown, to animal experimentation. Alternatives to it should be actively sought, its necessity in particular circumstances should be convincingly supported, its assumed animal models for human physiology and psychology should be carefully scrutinized, and cruelty to the animals involved should be avoided or at least minimized as far as possible.

When talking about the economics of fossil fuel consumption, we should not fail to take into account the so-called *externalities* connected with it. Externalities are unacknowledged and uncompensated costs imposed on people, animals, and the environment by this consumption. Greenhouse gas emissions and global climate change, particulates and other pollutants in the atmosphere, sludge from coal mines, ravages of the land from topping mountains to obtain coal, oil spills, pollutants in ground water and in waterways, acidification of the air and water, resultant health costs, and burdens on civic infrastructures such as streets and highways are examples.[10] Unless we recognize and demand payment for these externalities, we are not acknowledging the true economic impact of fossil fuel consumption. The long-range viability of our global economies requires us to attend promptly to the costs of these externalities.[11]

We should tax toxic emissions and other hidden economic costs, for example, and continue to seek for and implement alternatives to nonrenewable fossil fuels. We should not underestimate the possibility of developing viable substitutes for coal, oil, and natural gas. And one of these alternatives need not be nuclear *fission*, now that we are well aware of the problem of disposing of nuclear wastes and the hazard of meltdown and the spread of lethal radiation in nuclear fission power plants. Nuclear *fusion* may hold some promise, however, if it could be properly designed, made economical, and put to use. An exciting possibility for future renewable energy production is mastering the technique of photosynthesis that is routinely employed by plants.[12] There were times when widely available substitutes for draft animals or coal-fueled steam engines were not envisaged, and yet substitutes were later devised. We should begin to seriously consider and do something in earnest about the rapid rise of animal and plant extinction rates and the widespread effects of global climate change due to a marked extent to our current economic enterprises before it is too late and more irreversible damage on a global scale occurs.

Careful stewardship of all of nature is necessary both for the survival of endangered species, maintenance of a viable and sustaining natural environment, and our own future safety and security. Relatively short-range and restricted economic considerations should not cause us to lose sight of long-range economic and other consequences. It turns out that attending to the well-being of nonhuman animals and their species can have important spinoff effects for our economy and other aspects of our human well-being, as well as for the planet as a whole. In the final analysis, everything on the planet is connected and complexly interdependent to an extent that we are only recently and still slowly coming to recognize. Current economic factors do not stand alone. They should not be considered in isolation from other factors, be allowed to lord over them, or be detached from their impending consequences for the future.

2. The second objection is that it will be impossible to convince more than a small minority of people to adopt the outlooks, practices, and changes being recommended in this book, given that most of these stand in such sharp conflict with prevailing attitudes and beliefs. In other words, most of its recommendations are unrealistic, utopian, and pie-in-the-sky. They fly in the face of long-established and long-approved beliefs and practices. Failure to adopt them and carry them out to any significant degree is a foregone conclusion. The attainment of most of their goals is as unrealizable in practice as planning to travel to a distant city via flying carpet.

I can respond in these ways to this entrenchment of attitudes objection. We should not forget that seemingly unlikely sea changes can take place over finite periods of time if human beings put their minds to such changes and persist and persevere, as I observed in Chapter 4. The end of Apartheid in South Africa after a long period of brutal racial exclusion and prosecution, and revocation of the long-standing "Don't Ask, Don't Tell" policy regarding homosexuals in the United States military forces are examples that can be added to those mentioned there. Passage of the Animal Welfare Act in the United States in 1966 was accomplished in the face of substantial opposition at the time and was a step in the right direction, even though, and in spite of its subsequent amendments, it contains many exemptions and is not always effectively monitored and enforced. However, now that it has passed, the law and its applications can be steadily reevaluated and improved.

The point is this: what were originally a few voices crying out for change can over time swell into majority opinions and the consequent development of sweeping new laws, policies, and practices. Giving up in the face of disagreement and opposition, no matter how traditional, hoary, or well established the opposition may be or how entrenched certain attitudes and practices it reflects may be at present, is to guarantee that the needed changes will never take place. The future is open, and we should not be adamant or close-minded about what is or is not possible in the way of change. "Futures" in the past have been full of surprises and gone against the grain of many conventional expectations, and there is no good reason to think that our own future will be any different. Merely hoping that something will be so will admittedly not make it so, but hope combined with patience, imagination, and sustained effort can have that effect.

As I have emphasized before, making inroads on the offenses against nonhuman animals can be important progress, even though we do not attain the highest possible goals in their treatments. At the end of Chapter 9 of Plato's dialogue *The Republic*, Socrates admits that the dream of an ideally just, equitable, and well-ordered *polis* or city-state will possibly never become a full reality, but he insists that we should aspire toward it tirelessly as an ideal.[13] In similar fashion, we should be unflagging in our pursuit of the ideals I have set forth in this book. In some areas, incremental progress may be quite appropriate at least for a time, although in others the progress may need to be more sweeping and radical. As I have said before, moral (and religious) decisions are not always easy, and sometimes they can be inordinately hard. Moreover, formidable barriers often stand in the way of attainment of their goals. But citation of these facts is not a sufficient objection to trying to make the best decisions we can, to working unstintingly for the realization of their objectives, or for pursuing steady and meaningful approximations to the decisions' eminently worthy aims.

3. The third objection is that the point of view I am endorsing in this book is romantic, sentimental, and anthropomorphic, and thus ill-considered and extreme. It is no less extreme, on one end of the spectrum, than is complete indifference to the treatments of nonhuman animals, on the other end of that spectrum. The case being made for animal consciousness, feeling, and purpose is also distorted by unquestioning reliance on human experiences naively thought to be akin to those of animals. It is thus at bottom uncritically and flagrantly anthropomorphic in character. Nonhuman animals are radically different from human ones, and we should not carelessly impute the distinct qualities of our inner lives, with their acutely felt, linguistically and culturally refined pains, anxieties, frustrations, traumas, horrors, hopes, dreams, and ideals, to these animals. Moreover, nature is riddled with built-in predations, starvations, mutilations, deprivations, sufferings, and deaths, showing it not to be the Bambi-like realm of undisturbed peace and joy when left to its own devices that this book seems to be taking for granted.

My response to the charge of starry-eyed idealism and unrealism is that the view I am propounding does not overlook the differences between us and other animals, but it does insist that we recognize the similarities and take seriously their moral and religious implications. It is especially insistent on our taking into account the psychic lives of these animals and not treating them as mere instruments, implements, or automata or failing to do full justice to the inwardness that is a notable feature of all forms of life and comes into prominence with more complex forms of life. One extreme view sets humans over against the whole of nature, regarding everything in nature as subject without question to human uses and exploitations, no matter how trivial those uses and exploitations might be. This view is unapologetically *anthropocentric*, even though it avoids the charge of *anthropomorphism*. The other extreme betrays a simplistic, Peaceable Kingdom, hopelessly romantic outlook on nature.

My own view is quite different. If the wolf lies down with the lamb, the lamb will be torn to pieces and eaten. Nature's pervasive predations and routine sufferings are undeniable. It is replete with disasters such as wildfires, tsunamis, earthquakes, storms, floods, volcanic eruptions, droughts, and plagues that can sweep many forms of wildlife before them and radically alter ecosystems. Nature is marked by radical ambiguity when it comes to ordinary moral appraisals, but it is just this ambiguity that makes its marvels possible. Nature's creations and its destructions go hand-in-hand. For example, its evolutionary processes have brought widespread extinctions in their train and will no doubt continue to do so. And the destruction of older ecosystems and their inhabitants can make way for the creation of new systems with their own appropriate forms of life.

However, we have a choice whether or not to eat the lamb (and to attend to the welfare of the wolf). We have no right as humans to add needlessly or ruthlessly to the sufferings and deprivations of nature's forms of life, and we have every moral and religious reason to avoid doing so. A diagram exhibiting what I take to be the two extremes that should be avoided in thinking about these matters may help to make my own position clear. Here are the true extremes of the spectrum as I envision them.

Romantic, Sentimental, Anthropomorphic ↔ Indifferent, Manipulative, Anthropocentric

I do not champion or assume either of these extremes, and the objection is mistaken when it charges me with the extreme on the left side of the spectrum.

If compassion and care for the physical and psychic well-being of nonhuman animals are dismissively sentimental attitudes and actions, then the only remaining alternative would seem to be indifference to them altogether. One does not have to be hopelessly romantic to have such compassion and concern and want to do something about it. This is not extremism, but simple moral consideration. Without it, we become moral monsters, so far as our relations to nonhuman animals are concerned. If we do not deign to care for them, how long or to what extent will we care for one another? My basic position is really quite simple. We should reduce or eliminate animal pain and suffering whenever we can, and respect and support animals' distinctive natures and ways of life as fully as we can. But we must often do so on a case-by-case basis, recognizing not only that animals come in many different varieties, interests, needs, and susceptibilities, but also that situations for moral and religious assessment and choice vary.

Some cases, I have argued, are sufficiently clear-cut for me to argue for their general abandonment. Rodeos, circuses, zoos, and aquariums are four examples. Others exhibit varying shades of grey, such as animal experimentations. Here, mitigation rather than outright abandonment is in some and perhaps in many cases the more appropriate course. There are no easy solutions to moral conundrums such as the human population explosion or global climate change, but it is important that we make every effort to find seriously ameliorating solutions and put them quickly into practice—for our own sake as well as for the sakes of numerous animals and animal species the moral conundrums put in imminent danger. And our focus throughout should be on nonhuman animals and not just on us human ones. We are all—human and nonhuman—in this earthly system and situation together. We are part of a community or family of creatures, and we depend crucially on one another. The earth is our common, unimaginably complex, all-too fragile *oikos* or household.

4. The fourth objection is that I do not make an explicit choice between utilitarianism and rights theory, so my ethical philosophy and position are confusing and vague.[14] In the absence of such a choice and defense of it in relation to its alternatives, this book lacks the rigorous attention to technical theory, vocabulary, and argumentation that a convincing philosophical argument requires.

My response, as I have already indicated in the Preface, is that it is advisable to use aspects of each of the two theories when appropriate in different circumstances. A pluralistic moral outlook is appropriate, in other words, and rigorous, exclusive choice between the two theories or among all relevant, plausible theories is not necessary. I use the language of rights when I deem it appropriate, and that of utility in other contexts.[15] I have also brought in Aristotle's notion of *telos* in talking about the rights and welfare of nonhuman animals. An animal or group of animals has the *right* or entitlement to have its particular *telos* or mode of developing and living respected and protected by humans whenever possible. Another way of thinking about an animal's *telos* is to think about satisfaction of its natural preferences, needs, or characteristic ways of being, notions that can also be included under the heading of *utilitarianism*, as we saw in Chapter 3 when talking about Singer's preference utilitarianism. So utilitarianism, rights theory, and a focus on the Aristotelian notion of *telos* need not be radically contrasted with one another. In other words, there is no compelling reason to assume that all ethical considerations and situations must fit neatly into the scheme of a putative *summum bonum* or that it is necessary that they must all be finally conceived and dealt with in such a single-minded manner.

In fact, if we look at John Stuart Mill's utilitarianism, it is fundamentally Aristotelian in its appeal to the distinctive kinds of pleasure (namely, intellectual ones) that he believes humans to prefer when confronted with experience of and choice between them and more sensual pleasures. Aristotle's notion of humans as rational or essentially intellectual animals lurks behind Mill's drawing of this distinction, so crucial to his version of utilitarianism.[16] If we expand this notion of what forms of pleasure or satisfaction are most distinctive to particular sorts of animals in general, a *telos* view of their right to appropriate treatment and regard is brought into view. A pluralistic approach to the three theories is richer and more adequate than reliance on any one of them to the exclusion of the others.

And in taking a case-by-case approach to moral situations as they affect nonhuman animals, we might find one of the theories more helpful and insightful in one case and another one of them more illuminating in another. I do not feel the need of a lot of technical theory, vocabulary, and discussion to call credible attention to our need to recognize, respect, be responsible for, and hold in reverence nonhuman animals. There is certainly a place for that kind of investigation and analysis, but I do not think that it is necessary for the purposes of this book.

Principles and Prescriptions

I want now to summarize the major themes and conclusions of this book as a way of bringing it to a close. I do so in the form of an eightfold set of general principles and prescriptions relating to the treatment of nonhuman animals by human beings. I endorse the items of this list as a proponent of Religion of Nature, but I think that their general character and spirit, if not always their specific formulations, are consistent with the stances of many other religious and moral outlooks as well. There should thus be plenty of room here for effective cooperative endeavor among proponents of various religious and moral systems and approaches. The proposed principles and prescriptions are as follows:

1. We humans are not an isolated, self-sufficient species but integral members of an extensive community of species on earth.

2. We are unique creatures of nature, but our special gifts entail special responsibilities.

3. Large numbers of nonhuman animals are consciously aware in some degree, experience trauma and pain, and have important presumptive rights and distinctive modes of life.

4. We should refrain from inflicting unnecessary suffering or deprivation on these animals.

5. We should do all that we can to contribute to and ensure their prosperity and well-being.

6. We should reverence all creatures of earth and the whole of nature as holy ground, even as we give due recognition to the reality of nature's predations, disruptions, destructions, tragedies, and dangers.

7. We should be thankful for the privilege of being here on earth, even if only for the span of a lifetime, and of being able consciously to witness, reflect on, and marvel at nature's wonders.

8. We should rejoice in our ability to contribute with knowledgeable awareness and proficiency, both individually and

collectively, to the health and well-being of the earth and its creatures.

Incorporating and applying these principles and prescriptions to our relations with nonhuman animals would greatly improve their currently sorely mistreated and imperiled lot on this earth, and it would contribute decisively to our own sense of who we are and are capable of becoming as human beings.

We are not a ruling, self-sufficient species but one member of a huge network of species, each entangled with and crucially dependent on the others. We are but one kind of thou surrounded by a whole community of nonhuman thous who mutely and poignantly appeal to us for the reverential, respectful, responsible treatment they richly deserve. There are powerful religious and moral reasons for our responding to that appeal with the revolutionary attitudes and reformed modes of human life these reasons bring sharply into view. Most particularly, these reasons require that we hasten to replace an outworn but still all-too-prevalent attitude of arrogant, manipulative indifference toward our fellow thous with a new outlook and commitment of active justice, compassion, and love. This is our urgent challenge and opportunity in the contemporary world.

Notes

Preface

1. Edmund L. Pincoffs, *Quandaries and Virtues: Against Reductivism in Ethics* (Lawrence, KS: University Press of Kansas, 1986), 41.

Chapter 1

1. Charles Darwin, First Notebook (July 1837–February 1838), in *Darwin: A Norton Critical Edition*, ed. Philip Appleman (New York: W. W. Norton, 1970), 78.

2. See, for example, Crosby, *A Religion of Nature* (Albany, NY: State University of New York Press, 2002); "A Case for Religion of Nature," *Journal for the Study of Religion, Nature, and Culture*, 1/4 (2007): 489–502. *Living with Ambiguity: Religious Naturalism and the Menace of Evil* (Albany, NY: State University of New York Press, 2008); "Both Red and Green but Religiously Right: Coping with Evil in Religion of Nature," *American Journal of Theology and Philosophy*, 31/2 (2010), 108–23; and Chapter 8 of *Faith and Reason: Their Roles in Religious and Secular Life* (Albany, NY: State University of New York Press, 2011).

3. Andrew C. Revkin, "Who Made This Mess?" Review of Tim Flannery, *Here on Earth: A Natural History of the Planet*, in the *New York Times Book Review*, July 17, 2011, 16.

4. Galileo speaks in one of his writings of "this grand book, the universe, which stands continually open to our gaze. But the book cannot be understood," he goes on to insist, "unless one first learns to comprehend the language and read the letters in which it is composed. It is written in the language of mathematics, and its characters are triangles, circles, and other geometric figures without which it is humanly impossible to understand

a single word of it; without these, one wanders about in a dark labyrinth" (Galileo, *The Assayer* [1623], in Stillman Drake, *Discoveries and Opinions of Galileo* [New York: Anchor Books, 1957], 237–38).

5. In his *Meditations on First Philosophy*, 1642, Descartes draws a sharp distinction between two fundamental types of substance in the universe: thinking substance and extended substance. The latter, out of which he believes everything other than human beings on earth is constituted, he takes to be wholly amenable to mathematical analysis and explanation and thoroughly mechanical in its character. See Descartes, *Meditations*, Meditation II, in *The Philosophical Works of Descartes*, trans. Elizabeth S. Haldane and G. R. T. Ross, 2 vols. (Cambridge, UK: Cambridge University Press, 1967), I, 144–99.

6. Living animals were routinely beaten, manipulated, or vivisected by Descartes and others of his persuasion in their attempts to understand the animals' bodily functions. The cries animals emitted during these operations were regarded by the Cartesian researchers as nothing more than squeakings of the animal's machinery and were not thought to give evidence of anything like consciously experienced pain. See Peter Singer, *Animal Liberation: Updated Edition* (New York: HarperCollins, 2009), 201–2.

7. See the tree diagram and discussion of it Darwin provides in Part IV of *The Origin of Species*: Charles Darwin, *The Origin of Species* and *The Descent of Man* (New York, NY: Random House, The Modern Library, n.d.), 86–96.

8. Michael W. Fox, "What Future for Man and Earth? Toward a Biospiritual Ethic," in *On the Fifth Day: Animal Rights and Human Ethics*, eds. Richard Knowles Morris and Michael W. Fox (Washington, DC: Acropolis Books, 1978), 219–30, 227.

9. Donald Worster, *Nature's Economy: A History of Ecological Ideas*, 2nd ed. (New York, NY: Cambridge University Press, 1994), 192. I will be drawing on Worster's history of the checkered development of the discipline of ecology in natural science for much of the present section.

10. Worster, *Nature's Economy*, 295.

11. Paul Colinvaux points out that Elton did not have a satisfactory explanation of why the food chain is a pyramid, with prolific smaller organisms at the bottom and less and less numerous larger ones as the pyramid is ascended. Colinvaux's explanation is that at each level only a fraction of the caloric energy that the level below had not already used up can be extracted. "[W]ith this tithe," he notes, "the denizens of the upper levels must make their own bodies and fuel their lives. Which is why their numbers are only a fraction of the numbers below, which is to say, why they are rare." Paul Colinvaux, *Why Big Fierce Animals are Rare: An Ecologist's Perspective* (Princeton, NJ: Princeton University Press, 1978), 26.

12. An engaging book on this subject is the aptly titled *Eating the Sun: How Plants Power the Planet*, by Oliver Morton (New York, NY: HarperCollins, 2008).

13. Worster, *Nature's Economy*, 297.

14. Worster, *Nature's Economy*, 300.

15. Aldo Leopold, *A Sand County Almanac: And Sketches Here and There* (New York, NY: Oxford University Press, 1987), 204.

16. Eugene Odum, *Fundamentals of Ecology*, 3rd ed. (Philadelphia, PA: 1971), 8; quoted in Worster, *Nature's Economy*, 365.

17. Worster, *Nature's Economy*, 411.

18. Kuang-ming Wu, *Chuang Tzu: World Philosopher at Play* (New York, NY: Crossroad Publishing and Chico, CA: Scholar's Press, 1982), 136–37.

19. Colinvaux, *Why Big Fierce Animals are Rare*, 219, 218.

20. Worster, *Nature's Economy*, 429.

21. A thorough survey of the increasing involvement of world religions in ecological perspectives and responsibilities is Roger S. Gottlieb's *A Greener Faith: Religious Environmentalism and Our Planet's Future* (New York, NY: Oxford University Press), 2009.

Chapter 2

1. Donald R. Griffin, "From Cognition to Consciousness," in *A Communion of Subjects: Animals in Religion, Science, and Ethics*, eds. Paul Waldau and Kimberley Patton (New York, NY: Columbia University Press, 2006), 481–504, 481.

2. Griffin, "From Cognition to Consciousness," 498.

3. Marc Bekoff, "Wild Justice, Social Cognition, Fairness and Morality: A Deep Appreciation for the Subjective Lives of Animals," in *A Companion of Subjects: Animals in Religion, Science, and Ethics*, eds. Waldau and Patton, 461–480, 475.

4. I use here an apt phrase of Martha Nussbaum, in her discussion of Aristotle's ethics. See Martha Nussbaum, *The Fragility of Goodness: Luck and Ethics in Greek Tragedy and Philosophy* (New York, NY: Cambridge University Press, 1986), 321.

5. Evan Thompson, *Mind in Life: Biology, Phenomenology, and the Sciences of Mind* (Cambridge, MA: Belknap Press of Harvard University Press, 2007).

6. Thompson *Mind in Life*, 103–104.

7. Carl Safina, *Eye of the Albatross: Visions of Hope and Survival* (New York: Henry Holt and Company, 2002), 277–78). The italics are mine.

8. Thompson, *Mind in Life*, 161.

9. Thompson, *Mind in Life*, 237.

10. Thompson, *Mind in Life*, 162.

11. Jonathan Balcombe, *Second Nature: The Inner Lives of Animals* (New York: Palgrave Macmillan, 2010), 63.

12. Ned Block, "What Was I Thinking?" Review of Antonio Damasio, *Self Comes to Mind: Constructing the Conscious Brain* in *The New York Times Book Review*, Nov. 28, 2010: 21.

13. Balcombe, *Second Nature*, 66.

14. Bakoff, "Wild Justice," 465.

15. Terrence W. Deacon, *Incomplete Nature: How Mind Emerged from Matter* (New York, NY: W. W. Norton, 2012), 536.

16. Donald R. Griffin, *Animal Minds* (Chicago, IL: The University of Chicago Press, 1992), 13.

17. Balcombe, *Second Nature*, 47.

18. Frans De Waal, *Good Natured: The Origins of Right and Wrong in Humans and Other Animals* (Cambridge, MA: Harvard University Press, 1996), 96.

19. A fascinating article on the intelligence of a giant (40-pound, 5-foot-long) Pacific octopus is Sy Montgomery, "Deep Intellect: Inside the Mind of the Octopus," published in the November/December, 2011, issue of *Orion Magazine*. http://www.orionmagazine.org/index.php/articles/article/6474. Accessed November 14, 2011.

20. Lauritz S. Sømme, *Sentience and Pain in Invertebrates*, PDF version (Oslo, Norway, January 14, 2005), 36.

21. Sømme, *Sentience and Pain in Invertebrates*, 36.

Chapter 3

1. S. F. Sapontzis, *Morals, Reason, and Animals* (Philadelphia, PA: Temple University Press, 1987), 78.

2. Sapontzis, *Morals, Reason, and Animals*, 93–94.

3. The photograph was in the *New York Times Book Review*, November 28, 2010, 16, accompanying Geoffrey C. Ward's review of the third volume of Edmund Morris's biography of Roosevelt entitled *Colonel Roosevelt*.

4. Quoted in Henry F. Pringle, *Theodore Roosevelt* (Old Saybrook, CT: Konecky and Konecky, 1956), 243. Roosevelt's other side, his deep appreciation of and respect for every aspect of nature and the out-of-doors, is reflected in the fact that on one occasion, while visiting famed naturalist John Muir in what was to become Yosemite National Park, Roosevelt was able to recognize and name several bird species that Muir was unable to identify.

See Donald Worster, *A Passion for Nature: The Life of John Muir* (New York: Oxford University Press, 2008), 368.

5. Aldo Leopold, *A Sand County Almanac: And Sketches Here and There* (New York: Oxford University Press, 1989), 130.

6. See Evans, *With Respect for Nature: Living as Part of the Natural World* (Albany, NY: State University of New York Press, 2005), x.

7. Thompson, *Mind in Life*, 391.

8. Carl Safina, *The View from Lazy Point* (New York: Henry Holt and Company, 2011), 355.

9. In personal correspondence Conner objects to this way of putting the matter, saying "though we share much in common with animals, they do not reason as we do and many of their feelings and needs are not like ours." But my point is simply that many, though admittedly not all, of their feelings and needs are similar to our own. The rights I urge us to extend to animals are intended to take into consideration the distinct possibility (if not probability) that the particular nonhuman animal feelings and needs in question are closer in character to our own than we are sometimes prone or willing to recognize. Wondering about "the similarity between sharks and us," Safina muses that "[w]e name things based on differences, and sometimes similarities go unseen" (Carl Safina, *Eye of the Albatross: Visions of Hope and Survival* [New York, NY: Henry Holt and Company, 2002], 324). His observation about sharks is well worth pondering, and it has important bearing on the moral treatment of animals in general. While we should not ignore the differences, we should also be morally careful not to underestimate the similarities.

10. Safina complains that "[o]n the major issues affecting animals' future—endangered species, human poverty, human encroachment, forest destruction, ocean depletion, pollution, climate and ocean chemistry-change—giving individual animals rights offers no actual help. Animal-rights philosophy, so focused on 'sentience,' is itself unaware of ecological relationships and seemingly unconscious of the big picture" (Safina, *The View from Lazy Point*, 36). This statement sets up a false dichotomy, in my view. The rights approach I am advocating here requires concerted attention to preservation and melioration of the overall quality of the natural environments on which animals crucially depend. The list of rights I propose makes this point clear.

11. This right, like the others, can be overridden in particular circumstances. We may decide that it is in the best interest of a cat or dog population, for example, that it be kept within reasonable bounds by spaying or neutering so as to prevent widespread neglect, suffering, or starvation of these animals. In order that some may procreate and reproduce, the fertility of others must be prevented. Still, respect for the right in question will need

to be preserved and should continue to be regarded as the norm, only to be violated or restricted on the basis of compelling ethical considerations. The current restriction placed on the number of children parents are allowed to have in China, in order to curtail an excessive and overburdening population, is a human case in point. Is the latter a draconian solution to a widely recognized problem? Perhaps so, but the problem remains, and the general point is that particular rights may have to be overridden in particular cases so that other rights can be upheld.

12. Jeffrey A. Lockwood, *Grasshopper Dreaming: Reflections on Killing and Loving* (Boston, MA: Skinner House, 2002), 61. In personal correspondence Conner is right in noting in this connection that "the fate of most insects . . . [is] vastly beyond our control." But Lockwood's observation relates to the fates of those insects that may come within the span of our control and can thus be affected by our actions.

13. Bernard Rollin, "Ethics, Biotechnology, and Animals," in Waldau and Kimberley, eds., *A Communion of Subjects*, 519–32, 525.

14. "A Conversation with Peter Singer," in Hynn Höchsmann, *On Peter Singer* (Belmont, CA: Wadsworth, 2002), 83–92, p. 90.

15. Singer, "A Conversation," 85.

16. Singer uses this term in contrast with a hedonistic type of utilitarianism in "A Conversation," 90. See also his *Writings on an Ethical Life* (New York: HarperCollins, 2001), 133–35.

17. Martin Buber, *I and Thou*, trans. Walter Kaufmann (New York: Simon and Schuster, A Touchstone Book, 1996).

18. Phil Oliver, *William James's "Springs of Delight": The Return to Life* (Nashville, TN: Vanderbilt University Press, 2001), xiv.

19. For a recent development of this line of argument, see John F. Haught, *Is Nature Enough? Meaning and Truth in the Age of Science* (New York: Cambridge University Press, 2006). Contrary to religious naturalism in general and Religion of Nature in particular, Haught argues that nature is not enough.

20. Bron Taylor uses the term *dark green religion* to characterize "religion that considers nature to be sacred, imbued with intrinsic value, and worthy of reverent care." The term is useful, but Taylor includes much more under it than the Religion of Nature that is the central preoccupation of this book. Religion of Nature is an example of dark green religion as so described, but only one such example. A similar statement applies to the category of religious naturalism as a whole since Taylor does not confine dark green religion to naturalism but includes some kinds of supernaturalism as well. See Taylor, *Dark Green Religion: Nature Spirituality and the Planetary Future* (Berkeley, CA: University of California Press, 2010), ix, 14–16.

21. Philip K. Dick, *Do Androids Dream of Electric Sheep?* (New York: Ballantine Books, 1996).

22. As Singer suggests, it would surely not be beyond our scientific ability to design such highly selective baits if we had strong moral motivation and put our minds to the task. See Singer, *Animal Liberation*, updated edition (New York, NY: Harper Perennial, 2009), 233–34.

Chapter 4

1. Albert Schweitzer, *Reverence for Life*, trans. Reginald H. Fuller (New York: Harper and Row, 1969), 116.

2. Albert Schweitzer, *Civilization and Ethics*, 3rd ed. (London: Adam and Charles Black, 1949), 243.

3. This is the title of an essay in a collection of Schweitzer's writings entitled *Albert Schweitzer: An Anthology*, ed. Charles R. Joy (New York: Harper and Row, 1947).

4. In talking with one of my colleagues about the title and theme of this book, he warned that I would probably be accused of sentimentality and romanticism in undertaking to defend its basic ideas. He admitted that he was inclined in this direction, having heard a paper I had just presented in which I sketched and argued for some of the book's claims. A greater danger than sentimentality or romanticism, however, is that of being oblivious to all that we share with other creatures; of being insensitive to their right to life and to the pleasures, joys, and fulfillments appropriate to each of their types of life; and of having a calloused, indifferent attitude toward their experiences of unnecessary and unwarranted suffering and pain.

5. J. Claude Evans, *With Respect for Nature: Living as Part of the Natural World* (Albany, NY: State University of New York Press, 2005), 149.

6. Evans, *With Respect for Nature*, 157.

7. Evans, *With Respect for Nature*, 220.

8. A similar kind of deep nostalgia for a remote past suffuses Paul Shepard's book *The Tender Carnivore and the Sacred Game* (Athens, GA: The University of Georgia Press, 1999). Shepard sees hunting as a sacred ritual that reenacts the experiences of Paleolithic humans, thus bonding us with our evolutionary past and affirming and bringing home to us our close connections with nature.

9. Evans, *With Respect for Nature*, 164–70.

10. Joel Feinberg, "Human Duties and Animal Rights," in *On the Fifth Day: Animal Rights and Human Ethics*, eds. Richard Knowles Morris and Michael W. Fox (Washington, DC: Acropolis Books, 1978), 45–69, 64.

11. Dominion over the creatures can also be interpreted along the lines of a responsibility for humans to be caring stewards over nonhuman creatures of nature, but this interpretation carries the strong suggestion that humans

are set over against nature and entitled to preside over, monitor, and manage it from without rather than being integral parts of it. Thus interpreted, the concept still sets a wrong moral and religious tone so far as Religion of Nature is concerned. I do not think that the word *dominion* can be saved from such unfortunate and misleading connotations.

12. See Stuart Brown, "Do Fish Feel Pain? The Science Behind Whether Fish Feel Pain," FirstScience.com, September 5, 2003.

13. For discussion of a more recent study conducted by Joseph Garner and his associates that reached the conclusion that goldfish experience pain, see Harvey Black, "Underwater Suffering: Do Fish Feel Pain?" in *Scientific American*, September 17, 2009. http://www.scientificamerican.com/article. cfm?id=underwater-suffering-do-fish-feel-pain. Accessed May 18, 2012.

14. Evans, *With Respect for Nature*, 213–20.

15. Safina, *The View from Lazy Point*, 188, 139.

16. Safina, *The View from Lazy Point*, 114.

17. Safina, *The View from Lazy Point*, 229.

18. "A Conversation with Peter Singer," in Hynn Höchsmann, *On Peter Singer* (Belmont, CA: Wadsworth, 2002), 83–92: 87.

19. William James, "The Moral Philosopher and the Moral Life," in *William James: Essays on Faith and Morals*, selected by Ralph Barton Perry (Cleveland and New York: New World Publishing Company, 1992), 184–215: 194, 205.

Chapter 5

1. Martha C. Nussbaum, "Beyond 'Compassion and Humanity': Justice for Nonhuman Animals," in *Animal Rights: Current Debates and New Directions*, eds. Cass R. Sunstein and Martha C. Nussbaum (New York, NY: Oxford University Press, 2004), 299–320: 306.

2. David J. Wolfson and Mariann Sullivan, "Foxes in the Hen House: Animals, Agribusiness, and the Law: a Modern American Fable," in *Animal Rights: Current Debates and New Directions*, 205–33: 206.

3. Paul Waldau, *Animal Rights: What Everyone Needs to Know* (New York, NY: Oxford University Press, 2011), 37.

4. Jonathan Safran Foer's figure for factory-farmed *birds* alone throughout the world is fifty billion per year. "If India and China eventually start consuming poultry at the rate the United States does," he states, "it would more than double this already mind-blowing figure." See his *Eating Animals* (New York, NY: Little, Brown and Company, 2009), 137.

5. Foer, *Eating Animals*, 34.

6. Foer, *Eating Animals*, 34.

7. http://www.Feedstuffsfoodlink.com, September 2, 2011. Accessed October 12, 2011.

8. Foer, *Eating Animals*, 185.

9. Foer, *Eating Animals*, 187.

10. Foer, *Eating Animals*, 132–33; the quotation is on p. 133.

11. Foer, *Eating Animals*, 229–33.

12. Foer, *Eating Animals*, 50–51.

13. Foer, *Eating Animals*, 181–82; 231.

14. Nicholas D. Kristof, "Is an Egg for Breakfast Worth This?" the *New York Times*, April 12, 2012, A27.

15. See http://www.calfandheifer.org/?page=GoldStandardsIII.

16. See in this connection the August 5, 2011, interview between Chuck Jolley and Kurt Vogel in the Drovers Cattle Network. Vogel is a cattle handling expert who conducts seminars on animal welfare. Vogel rightly insists on the farming industry's obligation to present information in its advertisements and other media of communication that is true rather than misleading or false, and on the importance of its willingness to enter into more direct, ongoing, nondefensive dialogue with its critics. The critics must also, of course, be open to such dialogue. http://www.droverscattlenetwork. com. Accessed on this date.

17. Foer, *Eating Animals*, 193.

18. Quoted by Cornelia Dean, "Fishing Gear is Altered to Ease Collateral Costs to Marine Life," in the *New York Times* Reprint, August 22, 2011. http://www.nytreprints.com. Accessed on this date.

19. As I mentioned in Chapter 1, an excellent book dealing with the topic of growing ecological awareness and activity among a wide variety of religions is Roger S. Gottlieb's *A Greener Faith: Religious Environmentalism and Our Planet's Future* (New York, NY: Oxford University Press, 2009).

20. Jonathan A. Foley, "Can We Feed the World & Sustain the Planet?" In *Scientific American*, November, 2011, 60–65: 65.

21. See Kiera Butler, "Steak or Veggie Burger: Which is Greener?" http://motherjones.com/environment/2010/07. Accessed October 18, 2011.

22. Evans, *With Respect for Nature*, x, xv.

23. http://www.PewEnvironment.org/BigChicken.

24. Foer, *Eating Animals*, 58.

25. We would need to weigh in the balance the comparative ecological consequences of producing synthetic goods as over against leather goods. What chemicals are used? What natural resources are expended? What environmental effects are brought about? But we should not neglect to consider as carefully as possible the immediate consequences for animal welfare of producing and using leather goods.

Chapter 6

1. Thomas Berry, "Prologue: Loneliness and Presence," in *A Communion of Subjects: Animals in Religion, Science, and Ethics*, eds. Paul Waldau and Kimberley Patton (New York, NY: Columbia University Press, 2006), 6–10, 8.

2. Wesley J. Wildman comments in this way on the indispensable importance of non-discursive symbols in religion: "Religious objects are, at least sometimes, beyond expression in a more or less definitive way. Symbolic discourse is unavoidable in such cases. Preparing to perceive religious objects requires symbolism, forming beliefs based on religious perceptions requires symbolism, expressing these beliefs requires symbolism, and forging shared understanding through language and practices requires symbolism." Wildman, *Religious and Spiritual Experiences* (New York, NY: Cambridge University Press, 2011), 174–75.

3. We should not forget that issues concerning the moral treatment of animals are raised in non-factory farming and ranching as well. Practices of castration, branding, ear tagging, nose ringing, and de-horning without the use of anesthesia are examples. There is also the fact that animals are regularly bred and cared for in conventional farming and ranching in order to be slaughtered.

4. Paul Waldau, *Animal Rights: What Everyone Needs to Know* (New York, NY: Oxford University Press, 2011), 30.

5. Bernard E. Rollin, *Animal Rights and Human Morality* (Buffalo, NY: Prometheus Books, 1981), 137, 124–130.

6. Kenneth Shapiro, "Animal Experimentation," in *A Communion of Subjects: Animals in Religion, Science, and Ethics*, eds. Paul Waldau and Kimberley Patton (New York, NY: Columbia University Press, 2006), 533–43, 537, 542, 539.

7. Peter Singer, *Writings on an Ethical Life* (New York, NY: Harper-Collins, 2001), 45.

8. Thomas Berry, *The Sacred Universe: Earth, Spirituality, and Religion in the Twenty-First Century*, ed. Mary Evelyn Tucker (New York, NY: Columbia University Press), 2009, 82–85, 171.

9. Edward O. Wilson, *The Diversity of Life* (Cambridge, MA: Harvard University Press, 1992), 272.

10. News release of the International Union for the Conservation of Nature entitled "Another Leap Towards the Barometer of Life." http://www.iucnredlist.org/news/another-leap-towards-the-barometer-of-life. Accessed November 12, 2011.

11. Wildman, Religious and Spiritual Experiences, 218.

12. Both men are quoted in the news release of the International Union for the Conservation of Nature entitled "Another Leap Towards the Barometer of Life," cited above.

13. Paul R. Erlich, *The Population Bomb* (New York, NY: Ballantine Books, 1971). This is an expanded and revised edition of the book first published in 1968. The terms *population bomb* and *population explosion* were first used in 1954 on the cover of a pamphlet issued by the Hugh Moore Fund. The pamphlet was widely distributed over several years.

14. These figures are contained in an article "Seven Billion: Can the Population Keep Growing?" in *The Week* magazine, November 4, 2011, 19. See also Joel E. Cohen, "Seven Billion," *New York Times* Reprint, October 23, 2011. http://www.nytreprints.com. Accessed on this date. Cohen reports, "The United Nations Population Division anticipates 8 billion people by 2025, 9 billion by 2043 and 10 billion by 2083. India will have more people than China shortly after 2020, and sub-Saharan Africa will have more people than India before 2040."

15. Kierán Suckling, "7 Billion: More of Us, Fewer of Them," *The Huffington Post*, November 1, 2011.

16. Mireya Navarro, "Bringing Up the Issue of Population Growth," the *New York Times* Reprint, October 31, 2011. http://www.nytreprints.com. Accessed on this date. Navarro makes this statement in reporting on the views of Kevin Knobloch, president of the Union of Concerned Scientists.

17. Reported in Navarro, "Bringing Up the Issue of Population Growth."

18. Erlich, *The Population Bomb*, 162.

19. "Biggest Jump Ever Seen in Global Warming Gases." http://news.yahoo.com/biggest-jump-ever-seen-global-warming-gases-183955211.html Accessed November 14, 2011.

20. "Windows to the Universe: Warming of Polar Regions." http://www.windows2universe.org/earth/polar/polar_climate.html. Accessed May 23, 2012.

21. "Earth: A Graphic Look at the State of the World: Global Ecology." http://www.theglobaleducationproject.org/earth/global-ecology.php#2. Accessed May 23, 2012.

22. "Global Warming: Effects on Wildlife and Habitat." http://ww.nwf.org/Global-Warming/Effects-on-Wildlife-and-Habitat.aspx. Accessed November 15, 2011.

23. The three aspects of assurance, demand, and empowerment are critical features of all religious traditions, of course, and not just of Religion of Nature. I discuss these three aspects of Religion of Nature at some length in "Both Red and Green but Religiously Right: Coping with Evil in a Religion of Nature," *American Journal of Theology and Philosophy*, 31/2 (2010), 108–123.

Chapter 7

1. Carl Safina, *The View from Lazy Point: A Natural Year in an Unnatural World* (New York, NY: Henry Holt, 2011), 325.

2. The same thing is true of another one of Safina's books, *Eye of the Albatross: Visions of Hope and Survival* (New York, NY: Henry Holt, 2002), in which he, through the metaphorical eye of one fantastically far-ranging Laysan Albatross he calls Amelia, both celebrates the varied types and life styles of creatures of the air and sea and deplores the severe threats to them posed by destructive activities of human beings. The albatross is a deeply religious as well as a moral and literary symbol for Safina in this book.

3. *The Holy Scriptures According to the Masoretic Text: A New Translation* (Philadelphia, PA: The Jewish Publication Society, 1952).

4. Amos 5: 23–24, in *The Holy Scriptures According to the Masoretic Text.*

5. David Loy, *The Great Awakening: A Buddhist Social Theory* (Boston, MA: Wisdom Publications, 2003), 108. See also Loy's observation about the close connection between manipulation and alienation on 119. I am indebted to him for pointing out this connection.

6. "Such love," writes Loy, "is much more than a feeling," and it is "not just an insight or an intellectual awareness." It is rather "a mode of being in the world." *The Great Awakening*, 108.

7. Edward O. Wilson used the term *biophilia* in this sense in a work by this title (Cambridge, MA: Harvard University Press, 1984). He hypothesized that humans have deep, instinctive affiliations and feelings of connection with other natural beings, and that these affiliations and feelings are based in our genetic makeup.

8. Agricultural writer Ray Bowman reports that, according to U.S. Department of Agriculture estimates, castration of bulls intended for beef production amounts to approximately seven million procedures per year. He indicates that a study by the Iowa State University College of Veterinary Science concluded that while the benefits of castration include improved meat quality and fewer injuries in feedlots, castration of weaned calves is painful and stressful, which increases their susceptibility to diseases such as bovine respiratory disease. The findings of the study suggest that using pain relievers prior to castration in weaned calves is cost effective because the number of calves that will require antibiotics for pneumonia after castration decreases. The study, entitled "Effect of Oral Meloxicam on Health & Performance of Beef Steers Relative to Bulls Castrated upon Arrival at the Feedlot," was published online in the *Journal of Animal Science*. See Ray Bowman, "Pain relief at castration merited in calves." http://www.FeedstuffsFoodLink.com. December 19, 2011. Accessed December 20, 2011. It is important to note that the emphasis throughout in Bowman's report is on the cost effectiveness of castration procedures, not on the suffering of the animals when

these procedures are performed without the use of pain relievers. This is an inversion of the priority I am insisting on here.

9. According to a multi-national "Farm Perspective Study" conducted by BASF Corp., only 30 percent of six-thousand consumers said they would be willing to pay higher prices for food produced in a "green" or more sustainable way. See Rod Smith, "Consumer/Farmer Gap Evident." http://www. FeedstuffsFoodLink.com. December 7, 2011. Accessed December 12, 2011. Smith emphasizes in this article the importance of accurate communication between producers and consumers, and he rightly points to the need for consumers to understand their responsibility in seeking for more ecologically sustainable means of production. The same point would apply to consumers' avowed concern for the welfare of animals. Efficiency and lower costs, on the one hand, may be in conflict with ecological and moral considerations, on the other, and it is important that concerned consumers acknowledge and be willing to act in light of this fact.

10. See William D. Nordhaus, "Energy: Friend or Enemy?" in *The New York Review of Books*, October 27, 2011, 29–31. This article contains a diagram from the National Research Council showing that the external costs of electricity generation by coal are seventy percent of its market price, of generation by natural gas are nineteen percent, of heat production by natural gas are forty-two percent, and of transportation (primarily automotive gasoline) are twenty-five percent. See also the *New York Times* article by Paul Krugman, "Here Comes the Sun," November 6, 2011. Krugman calls attention to the sizeable hidden or external costs of "fracking" or injecting high pressure fluid into rocks deep underground to extract fossil fuels, and he points to the ever decreasing costs (especially when the external costs of fossil fuels are factored in) and increasing uses of solar panels as an alternative energy source to fossil fuels for the production of electrical energy.

11. A vivid example of such externalities is the consequence of converting Amazonian forests into cattle farms. "The cost of energy we would need to use to equal the air-conditioning and water supply functions of the Amazon forests," observes Gaia theorist James Lovelock, "is hundreds of trillions of dollars annually. This is far more than any replacement of forests by farms could yield." James Lovelock, *The Ages of Gaia: A Biography of our Living Earth* (New York, NY: W. W. Norton, 1995), 216; see also 226.

12. See David Owen, "The Artificial Leaf: Daniel Nocera's Vision for Sustainable Energy." *The New Yorker*, May 14, 2012, 68–74.

13. Plato, *Republic*, in The Collected Dialogues of Plato: Including the Letters, Edith Hamilton and Huntington Cairns, eds. (Princeton University Press, 1973), 819 (529b).

14. The classical contemporary defense of utilitarian theory as it relates to treatment of animals is Peter Singer's *Animal Liberation*, first published in 1975, and the equally classical contemporary defense of rights theory in this

regard is Tom Regan's *The Case for Animal Rights*, first published in 1983. See Singer, *Animal Liberation* (New York, NY: HarperCollins, 2009) and Regan, *The Case for Animal Rights* (Berkeley, CA: University of California Press, 2004).

15. Edward L. Pincoffs does an admirable and convincing job in arguing for a pluralistic, contextualist approach to the utilization of various ethical theories. See his *Quandaries and Virtues: Against Reductivism in Ethics* (Lawrence, KS: University Press of Kansas, 1986). I made mention of his book in the Preface.

16. See John Stuart Mill, *Utilitarianism*, ed. Oskar Priest (Indianapolis, IN: Bobbs-Merrill, 1957), 11–14. See also Aristotle, *Nichomachean Ethics*, trans. Terence Irwin (Indianapolis, IN: Hackett, 1985), 287 (1178a5): "For what is proper to each thing's nature is supremely best and pleasantest for it: and hence for a human being the life expressing understanding will be supremely best and pleasantest, if understanding above all is the human being. This life, then, will also be happiest."

Works Cited

"Another Leap Towards the Barometer of Life." News release of the International Union for the Conversation of Nature. http://www.iucnredlist.org/news/another-leap-towards-the-barometer-of-lfe. Accessed November 12, 2011.

Aristotle. *Nichomachean Ethics*, trans. Oskar Priest. Indianapolis, IN: Hackett, 1985.

Balcombe, Jonathan. *Second Nature: The Inner Lives of Animals*. New York, NY: Palgrave Macmillan, 2010.

Bekoff, Marc. "Wild Justice, Social Cognition, Fairness and Morality: A Deep Appreciation for the Subjective Lives of Animals." In *A Communion of Subjects: Animals in Religion, Science, and Ethics*, eds. Paul Waldau and Kimberley Patton, 461–80. New York, NY: Columbia University Press, 2006.

Berry, Thomas. "Prologue: Loneliness and Presence." In *A Communion of Subjects: Animals in Religion, Science, and Ethics*, eds. Paul Waldau and Kimberley Patton, 6–10. New York, NY: Columbia University Press, 2006.

———. *The Sacred Universe: Earth, Spirituality, and Religion in the Twenty-First Century*, ed. Mary Evelyn Tucker. New York, NY: Columbia University Press, 2009.

"Big Chicken: Pollution and Industrial Poultry Production in America." http://www.PewEnvironment.org/BigChicken.

"Biggest Jump Ever Seen in Global Warming Gases." http://news.yahoo.com/biggest-jump-ever-seen-global-warming-gases-183955211.html. Accessed November 14, 2011.

Black, Harvey. "Underwater Suffering: Do Fish Feel Pain?" *Scientific American Mind*, September 17, 2009. http://www.scientificamerican.com/article.cfm?id=underwater-suffering-do-fish-feel-pain. Accessed May 18, 2012.

Block, Ned. "What Was I Thinking?" Review of Antonio Damasio, *Self Comes to Mind: Constructing the Conscious Brain*. *The New York Times Book Review*, Nov. 28, 2010, 21.

Borenstein, Seth. "Biggest Jump Ever Seen in Global Warming Gases." http://news.yahoo.com/biggest-jump-ever-seen-global-warming-gases-18395521.html.Accessed November 14, 2011.

Bowman, Ray. "Pain Relief at Castration Merited in Calves." http://FeedstuffsFoodLink.com. December 19, 2011. Accessed December 20, 2011.

Brown, Stuart. "Do Fish Feel Pain? The Science Behind Whether Fish Feel Pain." FirstScience.com, September 5, 2003. Can be accessed at www. all-creatures.org/articles/ar-thescience.html.

Buber, Martin. *I and Thou*, trans. Walter Kaufmann. New York, NY: Simon and Shuster,Touchstone Book, 1996.

Butler, Kiera. "Steak or Veggie Burger: Which Is Greener?" http://mother-jones.com/environment/2020/07. Accessed October 18, 2011.

Cohen, Joel E. "Seven Billion." the *New York Times* Reprint, October 23, 2011. http://www.nytreprints.com. Accessed on this date.

Colinvaux, Paul. *Why Big Fierce Animals are Rare: An Ecologist's Perspective*. Princeton, NJ: Princeton University Press, 1978.

Crosby, Donald A. *A Religion of Nature*. Albany, NY: State University of New York Press, 2002.

———. "A Case for Religion of Nature." *Journal for the Study of Religion, Nature, and Culture*, 1/4 (2007): 489–502.

———. *Living with Ambiguity: Religious Naturalism and the Menace of Evil*. Albany, NY: StateState University of New York Press, 2008.

———. "Both Red and Green but Religiously Right: Coping with Evil in a Religion of Nature."*American Journal of Theology and Philosophy*, 31/2 (2010): 108–123.

———. *Faith and Reason: Their Roles in Religious and Secular Life*. Albany, NY: State University of New York Press, 2011.

Darwin, Charles. *The Origin of Species* and *The Descent of Man*. New York, NY: Random House, The Modern Library, n.d.

———. *Darwin: A Norton Critical Edition*, ed. Philip Appleman. New York, NY: W. W. Norton, 1970.

Deacon, Terence W. *Incomplete Nature: How Mind Emerged from Matter*. New York, NY: W. W. Norton, 2012.

Dean, Cornelia. "Fishing Gear is Altered to Ease Collateral Costs to Marine Life." the *New York Times* Reprint, August 22, 2011. http://www. nytreprints.com. Accessed on this date.

DesRoss. 2 vols. Cambridge, UK: Cambridge University Press, 1967.

De Waal, Frans. *Good Natured: The Origins of Right and Wrong in Humans and Other Animals.*Cambridge, MA: Harvard University Press, 1996.

Dick, Philip K. *Do Androids Dream of Electric Sheep?* New York, NY: Ballantine Books, 1996.

Drake, Stillman. *Discoveries and Opinions of Galileo.* New York, NY: Anchor Books, 1957.

"Earth: A Graphic Look at the State of the World: Global Ecology." http://www.theglobaleducationproject.org/earth/global-ecology.php#2. Accessed May 23, 2012.

Erlich, Paul. *The Population Bomb.* New York, NY: Ballantine Books, 1971.

Evans, J. Claude. *With Respect for Nature: Living as Part of the Natural World.* Albany, NY: State University of New York Press, 2005.

Feinberg, Joel. "Human Duties and Animal Rights." In *On the Fifth Day: Animal Rights and Human Ethics,* eds. Richard Knowles and Michael W. Fox, 45–69. Washington, DC: Acropolis Books, 1978.

Foer, Jonathan Safran. *Eating Animals.* New York, NY: Little, Brown and Company, 2009.

Foley, Jonathan A. "Can We Feed the World and Sustain the Planet?" *Scientific American,* November, 2011, 60–65.

Fox, Michael W. "What Future for Man and Earth? Toward a Biospiritual Ethic." In *On the Fifth Day: Animal Rights and Human Ethics,* eds. Richard Knowles Morris and Michael W. Fox, 219–30. Washington, DC: Acropolis Books, 1978.

"Global Education Project, The." Report of the National Wildlife Federation. http://www.theglobaleducationproject.org/earth/global-ecology.php#2. Accessed November 15, 2011.

"Global Warming: Effects on Wildlife and Habitat." http://www.nwf.org/Global-Warming/Effects-on-Wildlife-and-Habitat.aspx. Accessed November 15, 2011.

Gold Standards endorsed by the Dairy Calf and Heifer Association. http://www.clfandheifer.org/?page=GoldStandardsIII.

Gottlieb, Roger S. *A Greener Faith: Religious Environmentalism and One Planet's Future.* New York, NY: Oxford University Press, 2009.

Griffin, Donald R. *Animal Minds.* Chicago, IL: The University of Chicago Press, 1992.

———. "From Cognition to Consciousness." In *A Communion of Subjects: Animals in Religion, Science, and Ethics,* eds. Paul Waldau and Kimberley Patton, 481–504. New York, NY: Columbia University Press, 2006.

Haught, John F. *Is Nature Enough? Meaning and Truth in the Age of Science.* New York, NY: Cambridge University Press, 2006.

Höchsmann, Hynn. *On Peter Singer.* Belmont, CA: Wadsworth, 2002.

Holy Scriptures According to the Masoretic Text, The: A New Translation. Philadelphia, PA: The Jewish Publication Society, 1952.

James, William. "The Moral Philosopher and the Moral Life." In *William James: Essays on Faith and Morals,* selected by Ralph Barton Perry, 184–215. Cleveland and New York: New World Publishing Company, 1992.

Jolley, Chuck. "Five Minutes with Dr. Kurt Vogel." August 5, 2011. http://www.droverscattlenetwork.com. Accessed on this Date.

Kristof, Nicholas D. "Is Eating an Egg for Breakfast Worth This?" The *New York Times* Reprint, April 11, 2012. http://www.nytreprints.com. Accessed on this date.

Krugman, Paul. "Here Comes the Sun." The *New York Times* Reprint, November 6, 2011. http://www.nytreprints.com. Accessed on this date.

Leopold, Aldo. *A Sand County Almanac: And Sketches Here and There.* New York, NY: Oxford University Press, 1987.

Lockwood, Jeffrey. *Grasshopper Dreaming: Reflections on Killing and Loving.* Boston, MA: Skinner House, 2002.

Lovelock, James. *The Ages of Gaia: A Biography of our Living Earth.* New York, NY: W. W. Norton, 1995.

Loy, David. *The Great Awakening: A Buddhist Social Theory.* Boston, MA: Wisdom Publications, 2003.

Mill, John Stuart. *Utilitarianism*, ed. Oskar Priest. Indianapolis, IN: Bobbs-Merrill, 1957.

Montgomery, Sy. "Deep Intellect: Inside the Mind of the Octopus." http://www.orionmagazine.org/index.php/articles/article/6474. Accessed November 14, 2011.

Morton, Oliver. *Eating the Sun: How Plants Power the Planet.* New York, NY: HarperCollins, 2008.

Navarro, Mireya. "Bringing Up the Issue of Population Growth." The *New York Times* Reprint, October 31, 2011. http://www.nytreprints.com. Accessed on this date.

Nordhaus, William D. "Energy: Friend or Enemy?" *The New York Review of Books*, October 27, 2011, 29–31.

Nussbaum, Martha. *The Fragility of Goodness: Luck and Ethics in Greek Tragedy and Philosophy.* New York, NY: Cambridge University Press, 1986.

———. "Beyond 'Compassion and Humanity': Justice for Nonhuman Animals." In *Animal Rights: Current Debates and New Directions*, eds. Cass R. Sunstein and Martha C. Nussbaum, 299–320. New York, NY: Oxford University Press, 2004.

Odum, Eugene. *Fundamentals of Ecology.* 3rd edition. Philadelphia, PA: W. B. Saunders, 1971.

Oliver, Phil. *William James's "Springs of Delight": The Return to Life.* Nashville, TN: Vanderbilt University Press, 2001.

Owen, David. "The Artificial Leaf: Daniel Nocera's Vision for Sustainable Energy." *The New Yorker*, May 14, 2012, 68–74.

Pincoffs, Edmund L. *Quandaries and Virtues: Against Reductivism in Ethics.* Lawrence, KS: University Press of Kansas, 1986.

Plato, *The Collected Dialogues of Plato: Including the Letters*, ed. Edith Hamilton and Huntington Cairns. Princeton, NJ: Princeton University Press, 1973.

Pringle, Henry F. *Theodore Roosevelt*. Old Saybrook, CT: Konecky and Konecky, 1956.

Regan, Tom. *The Case for Animal Rights*. Berkeley, CA: University of California Press, 2004.

Revkin, Andrew C. "Who Made This Mess?" Review of Tim Flannery, *Here on Earth: A Natural History of the Planet*. The *New York Times Book Review*, July 17, 2011: 16.

Rollin, Bernard E. *Animal Rights and Human Morality*. Buffalo, NY: Prometheus Books, 1981.

———. "Ethics, Biotechnology, and Animals." In *A Communion of Subjects: Animals in Religion, Science, and Ethics*, eds. Paul Waldau and Kimberley Patton, 519–32. New York, NY: Columbia University Press, 2006.

Safina, Carl. *Eye of the Albatross: Visions of Hope and Survival*. New York, NY: Henry Holt and Company, 2002.

———. *The View from Lazy Point*. New York, NY: Henry Holt and Company, 2011.

Sapontzis, S. F. *Morals, Reason, and Animals*. Philadelphia, PA: Temple University Press, 1987.

Schweitzer, Albert. *Albert Schweitzer, An Anthology*, ed. Charles R. Joy. New York, NY: Harper and Row, 1947.

———. *Civilization and Ethics*, 3rd ed. London, UK: Adam and Charles Black, 1949.

———. *Reverence for Life*, trans. Reginald H. Fuller. New York, NY: Harper and Row, 1969.

"Seven Billion: Can the Population Keep Growing?" *The Week*. November 4, 2011, 19.

Shapiro, Kenneth. "Animal Experimentation." In *A Communion of Subjects: Animals in Religion, Science, and Ethics*, ed. Paul Waldau and Kimberley Patton, 533–43. New York, NY: Columbia University Press, 2006.

Shepard, Paul. *The Tender Carnivore and the Sacred Game*. Athans, GA: The University of Georgia Press, 1999.

Singer, Peter. *Writings on an Ethical Life*. New York, NY: HarperCollins, 2001.

———. *Animal Liberation: Updated Edition*. New York, NY: HarperCollins, 2009.

Smith, Rod. "Beak Trimming Benefits Welfare." http://www.FeedstuffsFoodLink.com, September 2, 2011. Accessed October 12, 2011.

————. "Consumer/Farmer Gap Evident." http://www.FeedstuffsFoodLink. com. December 7, 2011. Accessed December 12, 2011.

Sømme, Lauritz S. *Sentience and Pain in Vertebrates*. PDF version. Oslo, Norway, January 14, 2005.

Suckling, Kierán. "7 Billion: More of Us, Fewer of Them." *The Huffington Post*, November 1, 2011.

Taylor, Bron. *Dark Green Religion: Nature Spirituality and the Planetary Future*. Berkeley, CA: University of California Press, 2010.

Thompson, Evan. *Mind in Life: Biology, Phenomenology, and the Sciences of Mind*. Cambridge, MA: Belknap Press of Harvard University Press, 2007.

Waldau, Paul. *Animal Rights: What Everyone Needs to Know*. New York, NY: Oxford University Press, 2011.

"Windows to the Universe: Warming of the Polar Regions." http://www. windows2universe.org/earth/polar/polar_climate.html.

Wildman, Wesley. *Religious and Spiritual Experiences*. New York, NY: Cambridge University Press, 2011.

Wilson, Edmund O. *Biophilia*. Cambridge, MA: Harvard University Press, 1984.

————. *The Diversity of Life*. Cambridge, MA: Harvard University Press, 1992.

Wolfson, David J., and Mariann Sullivan, "Foxes in the Hen House: Animals, Agribusiness, and the Law: A Modern American Fable." In *Animal Rights: Current Debates and New Directions*, eds. Cass R. Sunstein and Martha C. Nussbaum, 205–33. New York, NY: Oxford University Press, 2004.

Worster, Donald. *Nature's Economy: A History of Ecological Ideas*. 2nd ed. New York, NY: Cambridge University Press, 1994.

————. *A Passion for Nature: The Life of John Muir*. New York, NY: Oxford University Press, 2005.

Wu, Kuang-ming. *Chaung Tzu: World Philosopher at Play*. New York, NY: Crossroad Publishing and Chico, CA: Scholar's Press, 1982.

Index